Italians

ITALIANS

David Willey

Photographs by
Fulvio Roiter

BRITISH BROADCASTING CORPORATION

To the memory of my Venetian grandparents,
Tullio and Gina, migrants both.

Published by
the British Broadcasting Corporation
35 Marylebone High Street, London W1M 4AA
ISBN 0 563 20312 9

First published 1984
Text © David Willey and the British Broadcasting Corporation 1984
Colour photographs © Fulvio Roiter 1984

Set in 11/14 Plantin by
Phoenix Photosetting, Chatham
Printed in Great Britain by
Mackays of Chatham Ltd
Colour illustrations printed by
Chorley and Pickersgill, Leeds
Colour separation by
Bridge Graphics Ltd, Hull

Contents

Preface

He who knows two cultures, lives two lives.
Chinese Proverb

After living in Rome for more than a decade reporting the daily doings of the Italians for the BBC, I felt I needed to set down on paper my view of a people with whom we British have a long relationship since our four hundred years of colonisation by the Romans.

We have developed special affinities through the visual and performing arts, through music, literature and politics, without mentioning the long-established custom of travel in Italy by our poets, writers, artists and men and women of sensibility. Nowadays up to two million people from the British Isles feel the call each year to travel south to Italy.

But their perception, and that of millions more who make the journey only in their imagination, tends to be distorted by false and even ridiculous stereotype images, and by the rapid changes that have taken place, and are continuing here during the last quarter of the twentieth century.

Even the Italians themselves are puzzled by the astonishing changes which have happened in their country since the Second World War. But it is my conviction that continuities with the past, whatever modern Italians may profess to the contrary, remain the key to understanding this complex country whose language and culture are still central to our Europe. The terrorist violence, the spread of mafia crime, the stresses and tensions of Italy in the seventies and eighties were the predictable result of the rapid progression from a poor agricultural society to a consumer-rich industrial and even post-industrial society.

The immediate cause of this book was the making of a series of documentary films for BBC Television. Ten Italians from widely differing backgrounds were selected from all over the peninsula to talk on film about their lives in the 1980s. I was asked to pull together this Italian social panorama, to set the scene against which this gallery of portraits should be viewed. Although each film explored the social context of its chosen character, its focus was necessarily narrow. I have taken a broader sweep and cast further afield in an attempt to equip both those readers who know Italy and those who do not with the necessary background to understand its inhabitants better.

I make no claim to present a definitive study of contemporary Italy, nor do I presume to answer that interviewer's stock question 'Whither Italy?' I have steered clear of politics in so far as this was possible, on the grounds that few Italians, let alone foreigners, understand the Byzantine system of government which operates in Rome, and that few of the people I talked to had much respect for their ruling classes.

My choice of interlocutors, as was the BBC-TV team's choice of characters for the film series, is purely personal. But I would like to thank the dozens of Italians who gave me their time and help during the preparation of this book and who are too numerous to mention by name for their kindness and understanding. I would also like to record my gratitude for the eighteen months hard work which went into the search for the selection and the filming of the characters for *Italians* by the series producer Jeremy Bennett, and his research assistants Virginia Bell and Anne Morrison.

David Willey
Rome, July 1984

ONE

No Choirs, Only Soloists

> For me it is morally salutary to be living in the midst of a sensual people about whom so much has been said and written and whom evey foreigner judges by the standard he brings with him.
>
> J. W. Goethe, on his arrival for the first time in Rome, 1 November 1786

An Italian of my acquaintance who went to live with her family in Cumbria in the mid-seventies was mildly surprised to be asked by the owner of the village shop, on learning of her nationality, whether her husband sold ice-cream or was a miner. He is in fact the director of a multinational chemical company.

Italians seem to me to be the least understood people in Europe. Their country is perceived in stereotype terms not just in England, but in France and West Germany, and on the other side of the Atlantic. The Germans run cover stories in their news magazines showing a revolver in a plate of spaghetti. The Americans delight in *Time* or *Newsweek* covers declaring that Italy is, once more, 'on the brink'.

The trouble is that the Italians themselves perpetuate junk ideas about their own country, in travel ads, by frequent reference to the Latin lover myth (Letin lover, by the way, in the vernacular), and by the uncritical assumption that opera, sunshine, good food, and other enjoyable commodities in life are somehow the monopoly of this relatively small, overpopulated Mediterranean peninsula.

Every year almost fifty million foreigners,[1] German hordes in the lead, converge on Italy in search of fine weather, art, wine, sex, culture, pizzas; pilgrims to a concept that belies the reality of a country which is now the world's seventh industrial nation and which, in the space of two generations, has undergone a radical social, cultural and economic transformation. The visitor's mental baggage of commonplaces is conditioned by two images which bear little relationship to the realities of the 1980s. The first is of more than a century of mass migration by impoverished Italians (the record year was 1913 when almost a million people left their native land in search of work and food). Italian migrants have made their mark in many parts of the world, but their image abroad has been as much conditioned by their lack of education as by their amiable disposition and adaptability to new lands. The second image is the

1. Foreign tourists visiting Italy in 1983 totalled 46,576,801, including W. Germany 10,366,053, France 7,891,903, UK 1,890,159, USA 1,717,411. Source: ISTAT.

residue of twenty years of Fascist rule, which only now, forty years on, the Italians are beginning to evaluate critically, instead of emotionally.

Seen from Italy, the perspective changes decisively. The migration for the purpose of survival of twenty-five million Italians (almost half the country's present population) after 1870, and the Mussolini interlude, are but two episodes in a bimillennial history in which it is the varied experience that counts. Italians have survived practically every conceivable form of good and bad government known to mankind, starting off with the ancient Greeks and Romans, so they can afford to regard with a certain world-weariness the antics and inadequacies of their present ruling classes.

The historical landmarks that Italians themselves regard as important are not necessarily the same as those selected by foreigners. Giuseppe Garibaldi, the nineteenth-century hero of Italy's unification, the Risorgimento, came out way ahead of today's leaders or of Benito Mussolini in a recent survey[2] of Italians' opinions about themselves. The poet and ideologue of the Risorgimento, Giuseppe Mazzini, was judged to be much more *simpatico* than any current political figure, while the nineteenth-century statesman Camillo Cavour was considered twice as *simpatico* as Mussolini.

Over ninety per cent of those polled in all age groups and of both sexes said they were glad to have been born Italians, and would not wish to live in any other country. The tiny minority who would have preferred to have been born and brought up elsewhere looked mainly towards Britain, the United States and West Germany.

The great exodus in search of new lives and jobs abroad has now come to an end. The trickle outward bound is balanced by the return of former migrants and by the arrival of hundreds of thousands of third-world citizens from Africa and Asia (many of them illegal residents) who seek in the Italy of the eighties the consumer Eldorado and the land of opportunity that previous Italian generations found in the Americas and in Northern Europe.

Francesco Tinelli is one of those who decided to return home, a victim of economic recession in Northern Europe. I met him in the mayor's office in the small agricultural town of Montemilone (pop: 2,660) in the province of Basilicata in the heel of Italy. After seventeen years of voluntary exile as a factory worker, first in West Germany, then in a Luxembourg steelworks, he decided at the age of forty-two to bring his wife and six children back to Italy. There were no more jobs going in Luxembourg when he was laid off and he calculated that with no more rent to pay (he owns a three-room house and a hectare of land in Montemilone) and lower living costs, he would be better off at home. But he is still swimming against the tide, as there are no jobs in Montemilone either. He had just done fifteen days' casual labour for the comune, but needed 200 days of manual work to get by. The local subsistence economy enabled him to grow enough to eat for his family. His children, who all

2. Monitorskopea Survey for *La Repubblica*, February 1984.

speak fluent German, were finding it hard to settle, and there is no German language instruction at the local school. Francesco Tinelli returned to a peasant culture in a dying community. Within the past twenty years Montemilone lost almost half its population through migration and is now a town of old people. However there is a reverse side to the medal. In prosperous Bergamo, 1,000 kilometres to the north, I met Fernanda Ghilardi, the owner of a shirt factory who was doing very nicely indeed, with a brand new plant, plenty of orders, a flair for design and selling, and no trouble at all in marketing the 5,000 shirts she produces every day, anywhere from Los Angeles to Sicily. She told me that her workers are rather well paid, and enjoy seven weeks, two hours and forty minutes' paid holiday every year. She also told me that she has trouble getting the girls who cut the cloth and sew the shirts to work overtime. 'I tried to tempt one of them with the fact that she could buy herself a fur coat with the extra money. But she told me she has two fur coats already, one jacket-length mink and one long ocelot.'

Consumer Italy is sometimes hard to believe in, as the successor to what used to be, within the living memory of many millions of Italians, a very poor country indeed. Conspicuous consumption is not limited to the prosperous, productive areas of the country. The streets of economically depressed cities such as Palermo and Naples are as clogged with traffic as are Milan and Turin, such is the overwhelming desire of all Italians to own a motor car. Eighty per cent of families own one car and twenty per cent own two – in Britain forty-eight per cent are one-car owners and thirteen per cent two-car owners. While in Naples in the late seventies to investigate the outbreak of a mysterious epidemic which was killing babies, particularly those of poor families, I was struck by the presence in even the most pestilential and damp and overcrowded homes that I visited of a colour television set, generally with the largest available twenty-six-inch screen. Washing machines and refrigerators are considered necessities by housewives in the poorest villages.

Although infant mortality figures have dropped dramatically this century, and have now fallen to a level comparable with the rest of Western Europe, Don Vito, a priest I met in Puglia, told me that as recently as the 1960s he remembered conducting the funerals of at least two dozen infants each summer at Anzi, the mountain village near Potenza in Southern Italy where he was parish priest.

Italy's vital statistics tell the story of the enormous changes that have taken place this century. Italians can expect to live almost twice as long as their immediate forebears. Illiteracy, which officially stood at fifty per cent at the beginning of the century, and was probably even greater in reality, has fallen to negligible levels, mainly among the aged, although as in most other Western European countries there remains a stubbornly sizeable proportion of people who have passed through the school system, yet learnt little from it. Italians are marrying less, conceiving fewer children, eating more meat, and are beginning to eat less spaghetti, just as pasta consumption is rising in the rest of the industrialised world.

The dietary changes noted this century tell the story of the transition from subsistence-level agriculture, to an industrial market economy. Meat consumption has increased five times and the meat import bill is one of the heaviest items in Italy's Balance of Payments deficit; Italians are drinking twice as much milk, consuming ten times as much sugar as at the turn of the century. Maize consumption has dwindled by two-thirds as the habit of eating polenta, formerly a staple over large areas of northern Italy, has declined in favour of faster cooked foods. It takes an hour's constant stirring to prepare a good plate of steaming polenta, and there are not so many ready hands around nowadays, in the shape of small children or grannies, to stop the polenta burning.

Francesco Longo, a Sicilian fisherman, was born into that poor Italy like his father and grandfather before him, who also made their living from the sea. During his eighty years he has lived through all these dramatic changes, and told me, sitting in his modest, spotless house, fronting right onto the beach overlooking the straits of Messina, that Italy today 'is better off than America!'

'America has arrived here! Such prosperity! Almost everyone has a job. You can't grumble. Everyone has houses worth fifty or a hundred million lire. People own a boat, a house, and have a job. And even the women work!'

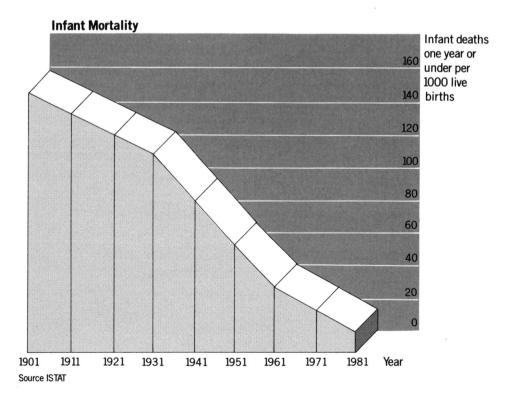

Infant Mortality

Infant deaths one year or under per 1000 live births

Source ISTAT

Even for the succeeding generation to Francesco, the changes that have occurred in the period during which they grew up, married and had children have been so far-reaching that Italian sociologists, political scientists and economists are still scratching their heads trying to find out what it all means. The CENSIS Foundation is an officially-sponsored research institute which publishes an annual report on social developments. Giuseppe De Rita, the head of CENSIS, sees Italy today as 'a happy ant-heap where everyone is running about and no-one is in control'.

Life expectancy

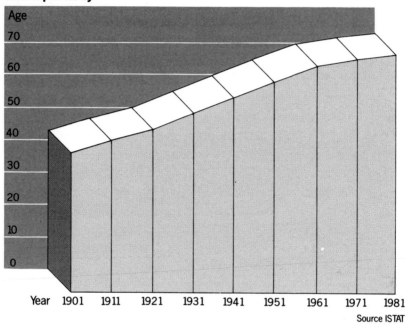

Source ISTAT

Illiteracy

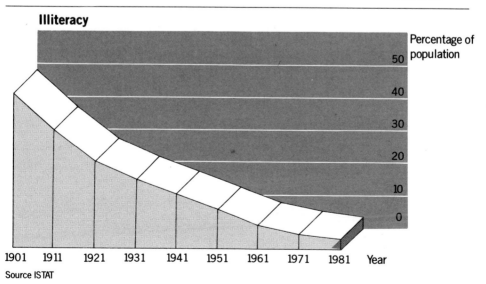

Source ISTAT

His latest report[3] reveals a prosperous society in which sixty per cent of families own the house they live in, where the rich and the moderately wealthy are increasing their share of national wealth, but the poor remain a substantial number, twenty-eight per cent of families at the last count.

De Rita says: 'Fragmentation reigns, multiplicity of behaviour, cultural polytheism.

'Once upon a time the job market was sharply divided between those who had guaranteed jobs and the desert of the unemployed. Now the barrier has become blurred. Moonlighting is imposed on top of official work. Millions of workers move about (nearly three million Italians change jobs each year and almost two million their place of residence) or work part-time. The system is moving very rapidly.

'Take the role of the cities. Once Rome was the administrative capital, Milan, the centre for service industries, and Naples, the capital of the centre-south. Now these neat divisions have been shot to pieces, new centres are developing in the south, Bari is economically more powerful than Naples, Catania than Reggio Calabria. In northern Italy new development areas based on service industries are emerging. Padua and Vicenza in the Veneto, and Bologna and Modena in Emilia.

'It is light years away from reality to believe you can control the economy by traditional means today. Take money supply for example. The situation is much more complex today than in the sixties or seventies when a governor of the Bank of Italy simply had to pull levers to start a credit squeeze which had an immediate effect on the economy.

'Even demographically speaking there is an overlap of behaviour. You cannot talk meaningfully any more about the first, second and third ages. In each age band there are new divisions, the pensioner who goes on working, the ninety-year-old living in hospital.

'And who can bring a common denominator to the problems and behaviour of those between fifteen and twenty-nine?

'Even politics is rent by subdivisions. Look at the list of candidates in the 1983 elections. You have everything there, pensioners, local groups, ethnic groups, even an ambiguous lot called "Campania Felix" composed of old and new Neapolitan mafia families together with their old and new brothers in jail. No one has yet unravelled that particular piece of string!

'A return to law and order, the handing over of powers to some person or institution in the name of efficient decision-making is just a dangerous illusion. We in Italy are looking for a new cultural, social and political leadership that cannot stop at a simple recovery of authority. I realise that this is going to cause a crisis for researchers like us as much as for those who have a concept of politics as something which expresses the pre-eminence of the State, Will, Authority, Reason or Party.

3. CENSIS XVII Rapporto 1983, Franco Angeli Editore.

'Whether we like it or not the truth is that multidimensional Italian society is not a pyramid on which anyone can sit at the top. No one can at the same time look at the sides of the pyramid and scan the horizon to find out where we are heading. Fragmented society is like a skyscraper with many floors. Those who are on the top floor see only one façade at a time and only part of the horizon. To know what's going on below you have to look at the other floors, see how they intercommunicate, get to know how the lifts work, and the telephones, and the wiring . . .'

While Professor De Rita examines the wiring, other researchers have been trying to decide whether or not Italians are a happy people. According to a report commissioned by the Common Market, Italians are the least happy people in Europe, beaten only by the Greeks in their sense of pessimism. Only six out of every 100 Italians questioned in what purported to be a serious survey said that they could consider themselves to be truly happy.

A leading psychoanalyst, who has had stretched out on his couch some of the biggest names in high finance, and members of some of the best-known families in Italy, believes this is all nonsense.

Professor Cesare Musatti, doyen of Italy's followers of Freud, said: 'Italians say they are extremely unhappy, but in fact they are one of the most contented people on earth. If you ask them, they'll say that everything's going to pieces, and that nothing works in this country. But things are rather good, we eat better than practically anywhere else in the world; there are isolated pockets of depression and relative poverty, but this presumed unhappiness of Italians seems like a put-up job to me. The National Budget is in deficit, but people simply don't care because they understand very well that you can perfectly well live with inflation.'

Anthropologist Luigi Lombardi Satriani took a different view. 'We in Italy follow a tradition that considers happiness a marginal factor; it's a penitential, gloomy vision which has its origin both in Catholicism and in Marxism, the main pillars of our cultural models. (D. H. Lawrence was of the same opinion. Writing in 1913 he said: "The Italian people are called 'the Children of the Sun'. They might better be called 'Children of the Shadow'. Their souls are dark and nocturnal.")

'I think the Italians are really unhappy,' Lombardi Satriani went on. 'A sense of insecurity is growing because there is no longer any attachment to models of social reference. And above all among the young there's a wide gap between their own dreams and the real possibilities of adult life.'

Sociologist Sabino Acquaviva believes instead that Italians are simply more inclined to complain than other nations.

'I believe that people are fairly happy in small and medium-sized towns, but in the big cities where life is a continual struggle for survival, the situation is much less rosy. Italians have lost their points of reference. Once upon a time we had a precise goal: to construct a society of saints (in the case of the Church) or a society of equals (in the case of Marxism). Now these lofty projects no longer exist and our anxiety is growing.'

The sense of stress in Italy of the eighties is understandable when one considers how late the industrial revolution hit the country. The Alfa-Romeo car factory near Milan, scene of some of the most important developments in the history of the Red Brigade terrorist movement during the seventies, only went over from artisan methods of car assembly to a modern production line at the beginning of the sixties, that is to say almost fifty years after Henry Ford started up his assembly lines for the Model T in the United States. What has taken many decades to accomplish in the building of a modern industrial state in Britain or the United States has been compressed into a much narrower time-span in Italy resulting in understandable stress, confusion and misunderstandings. However, one must also take into account the legacy of an extremely rich and varied history extending back not just to the beginnings of the Italian State in the last century, but to the Renaissance, to the temporal rule of the Papacy, to the Middle Ages, and of course to Ancient Rome, not to mention Magna Graecia.

Thus while Italy may have come late to the production line, it is also useful to remember that it came early to the world of international commerce and manufacture. Contracting out, the industrial method in use today in the prosperous small textile town of Prato near Florence, dates back to the thirteenth and fourteenth centuries, not to excesses of nineteenth-century proletarian exploitation denounced by Karl Marx.

Mario Becchi, fifty-five, who with his brother and nephew runs three looms that he owns himself in his own village workshop near Prato, forms part of a complex industrial process first organised by the mediaeval cloth guild, the *Arte della Lana* in 1351. True, Mario is a convinced member of the Italian Communist Party, but he is also jealous of his privileges as an independent craftsman. Shouting above the clatter of his shuttles he said: 'I wouldn't change this for an ordinary factory job for any reason. We are free here, not watching the clock, and the whole family is involved, my wife as well. Bosses only exist, you know, because we create them!' The statutes of the *Arte della Lana* regulated the complex relationship between sorters, washers, woolcombers, carders, spinners, weavers, fullers, dyers and finishers in a capitalist system that has survived for seven centuries, as it continues to give satisfaction to artisans and profits to businessmen. We shall be returning to Prato in Chapter Three.

Demographic decline is something quite new for Italians to experience, although it is now a widespread phenomenon in western Europe. Since 1964, the number of babies born each year has dropped quite regularly and dramatically from over a million to just over half a million. In northern Italy there are now actually more deaths than births each year; the population has been decreasing in north-west Italy for the past five years and in the north-east for three successive years. Overall the population remains more or less steady as a higher birthrate in the south offsets demographic losses in the north.

The reasons for the fall in the birthrate are still being debated, but it represents a far-reaching social and cultural change, affecting not only the family (the one-child family is now the norm in Italy) but also patterns of consumption, school planning, and adults' view of their future. Rome University is giving a new course on the prospects for nuclear disarmament and the potential horrors of nuclear warfare, while more than two million Italians paid to see the American TV film on the nuclear holocaust *The Day After* at the cinema within two weeks of release in 135 towns and cities. The film made more money at the box office than any other film in the history of the Italian cinema, and this at a time when cinema attendances had been in decline for years in accordance with a long-term trend.

The flight from the land has been quite as dramatic as the fall in the birthrate. Since 1960, more than four million Italian workers have abandoned farming. Most of them found alternative jobs in service industries which now account for just over half the total workforce. Industrial employment has been rising only very slowly after the economic boom of the fifties and sixties. The shift away from the land has not however been simply geographical. Former peasant culture and family organisation translated to the towns and cities has led to a cross-fertilisation between urban living and peasant skills.

Pipe smoking, thirty-three-year-old Mauro Fiammenghi is a quality controller at the huge sprawling Alfa-Romeo car factory, the one which only went over to a modern production-line in 1961. Physically he looks like Italy's counterpart to Lech Walesa. He's now a fully integrated member of industrial society, a keen trade unionist shop steward, but his lifestyle reflects his family origins, which he is keen to transmit to his children.

Mauro comes from a little village in the province of Cremona: 'a peasant village, really, a village of the plain where they rear animals and work in the fields,' was how he described it. His wife Caterina comes from a mountain family with different traditions, but country folk all the same. Caterina's parents' house in the foothills of the Alps where she grew up is now the weekend family retreat, '*una fuga felice*' (a happy refuge) is how Mauro described it. Every Saturday and Sunday the Fiammenghi family leave their small rented flat in an anonymous Milan street to return to their roots.

'On Saturday and Sunday the problems are quite different from those you get in the city. There are different bonds of affection too among people, they are more friendly, and that's not something which only I feel, the whole family feels it too. The two boys look more cheerful, not just because they don't have to go to school, but because they know that for two days we shall be living in a completely different way, healthier, more relaxed.

'We spend our summers there too, and we have extended the house with some weekly sacrifices. [Mauro's weekly take home pay is about £90 sterling per week at 1984 exchange rates.] I spend time cultivating my small vineyard and the fruit trees. Among other things I am teaching my son Cristian all the little secrets of how to grow things, and we are also keeping alive the memory of the old grandparents.'

The real economic strength of northern Italy lies not so much in big industry, like Alfa-Romeo, or Fiat, but the still proliferating small-scale commercial and industrial enterprises, usually family run. People whose families used to be farmers have brought to their new environment deep-rooted traditions which make them particularly well equipped for their new lives. The traditions of keeping ownership within the family, of pooling incomes, of managing and allocating jobs within the family, coupled with families' well-known capacity for thrift and saving, makes these firms particularly resilient and flexible, and able to meet practically any sort of crisis.

Take the success story of the Benetton family from Treviso, near Venice, who in less than twenty years have built up from scratch a business which is now the world's largest producer of woollen knitwear. Giuliana Benetton, who remembers that as a little girl at school she had a passion for knitting while the other children were playing games, helps run a family industrial empire with ten factories, 2,500 shops, and a worldwide export business. Giuliana, forty-five, looks after the design, while Gilberto, forty-two, runs administration and finance, Carlo, thirty-eight, is production chief, and Luciano, forty-seven, the eldest, controls the thriving export trade.

The Benettons' father, who was a lorry driver, died when Luciano was only ten. Now the family operates from a beautifully restored seventeenth-century villa decorated with frescoes and antiques which was once the summer home of a Venetian nobleman. Yet a hundred yards away from this ancient splendour lies a brand-new factory equipped with the latest hi-tech machinery for responding to computer orders flowing directly into the headquarters from terminals in shops all over Europe. Benetton claims to be able to respond instantly to changes in fashion demand as each sale in each shop anywhere in the world is rung up and transmitted automatically to Italy giving colour and size. So a sudden spurt in the sales of purple pullovers in Paris today, or red denims in Oxford Street tomorrow, can be the signal for rushing new supplies or switching stocks elsewhere. Although non-family members are now having to be brought in to help top management, the basic philosophy of the Benettons is still to keep their payrolls as slim as possible, to subcontract production, and to franchise retail outlets rather than to invest too heavily in shops themselves. The family owned and run business also has a totally different attitude to the question of their employees' trade union rights from that of the non-family enterprise.

Giovanna Mazzocchi, another highly competent business lady, who runs a profitable publishing empire in Milan was absolutely frank to me about the criteria for selecting the 180 staff who run her specialised business.

'We have no union problems here,' she said with some emphasis as we had lunch in the architect-designed canteen where employees and the boss eat together. 'I tell my department heads to be very careful in selecting staff as it's so difficult to sack them. Anyone with strong political views is out for a start. Work is no place for politics. You can do that in your own time, but certainly not bring it in here.'

Some fairly radical legislation was brought into force to protect workers' rights after the turbulent events of the 'Hot Autumn' of 1969 – the workers' revolt which was sparked off by the student rebellion of 1968. But the small average size of businesses in Italy and the outlawing of the 'closed shop' ('all activities and agreements are declared null which subordinate employment to the condition that a worker belongs, or does not belong to a trade union') mean in practice that Italian unions are weaker than their British counterparts. They also lack strike funds to sustain prolonged stoppages, which means that strikes in Italy tend to be short and symbolic, although not necessarily less effective.

One of the main difficulties in writing about Italians is that for ethnic, geographical and historic reasons they are such a varied and individualistic people that you must first of all answer the question 'which Italians?' if you want to make sense.

In the course of my travels inside Italy for the purposes of this book, I have ranged all the way from Rain-in-Taufers, a remote Alpine village in the snows perched five thousand feet up on the Austrian border, where German is the main language, to Mazara del Vallo, a fishing port on the south-west coast of Sicily where you can hear Arabic spoken. Mazara looks out to North Africa and has a Kasbah populated by three thousand Tunisians. The Arabs landed here early in the ninth century to begin their conquest of Sicily. I suppose you could call this the equivalent of travelling in Britain from Land's End to John O'Groats.

Between these two extremities lie dozens of formerly autonomous towns and cities which until very recently had little in common, and some of which indeed for long centuries were frequently at war with each other. In the monumental Campo Santo, the cemetery in Pisa, two massive sets of rusting chains hung on a wall are a vivid reminder of these wars and battles. The chains used to close off the harbour against the enemies of what used to be one of Italy's independent maritime republics. One set of chains was carried off as a battle trophy by the armies of Pisa's arch-rival Genoa, and a replacement set was later captured by the Florentines. The chains were finally sent back to Pisa hundreds of years later in the middle of the last century to celebrate the political unity that Italy had lost more than a millennium before. The number of Pisans taken prisoner by the Genoese in a naval battle in 1284 which marked the end of Pisa as a great naval power was so great that the shame of the defeat passed into a local saying, still in use in Tuscany today: 'If you want to see Pisa, go to Genoa'.

When Italy became a united country under the Royal House of Savoy in 1861, it barely had a common language. Not more than three per cent of the population (25 million at that time in comparison with the 56 million counted at the last complete census in 1981) spoke correct Italian (Tuscan variety). The remainder communicated in dialects which were often incomprehensible in other parts of the peninsula.[4]

This sometimes led to tragic results. Under a conscription law introduced by the Piedmontese in Sicily, young Sicilian men were forced into the army for periods of up to eight years. Cases are on record of conscripts being shot for refusal to obey orders of officers who spoke what to them was a foreign language.

Almost a century later, 1951, a national survey revealed that standard Italian was still being spoken by only 18 per cent of the population. By 1982, the number of those habitually speaking in local or regional dialect to their families or in their daily occupation had fallen to less than half the population.

But the latest research in Sicily indicated that fifteen Sicilians in a hundred still communicate exclusively in dialect. Paradoxically it was Sicilians of modest education brought up speaking dialect at home who were most keen on their own offspring learning correct Italian, while graduates seemed more anxious to encourage and preserve for their children the use of their native Sicilian.

The press, television and radio and compulsory schooling have all helped to spread the use of standard Italian, but it's worth noting that one of Italy's greatest twentieth-century actor-playwrights, Eduardo de Filippo, wrote and performed in Neapolitan dialect which forms an essential comic element in his plays.

Mario Nervegna from Parma (the town which gave its name to Parmesan cheese as well as inspiring Stendhal to write one of his greatest novels) is the managing director of a big spaghetti industry, with headquarters in Naples. As an efficient, business-oriented northerner having to deal daily with southerners of quite different temperament, he has had cause and time to reflect upon the differences between Italians.

As we drove down the motorway, the Autostrada del Sole, from Rome on the way to inspect his factories making 104 varieties of pasta, we overtook a car bearing Swiss number-plates.

'The unity of Italy is a complete abstraction,' he suddenly remarked. 'I once passed a Swiss-registered car going down here, and then realised that the people inside were not Swiss, but Sicilians on their way home from work in Switzerland. And then I asked myself what difference does it really make to me that they were Sicilians instead of Swiss?

4. See Tullio de Mauro *Storia linguistica dell 'Italia unita*, Bari 1972, P. 43.

'Even today being an Italian is a philosophical concept rather than a practical matter. It's sad to say, but it's true. Italy has had a very disconnected past. The province of Vicenza, for example, is very different from the neighbouring province of Padua. And let's not think how different both are from Naples!'

The original Italians, the *Itali*, were a tribe who inhabited the area now known as Calabria, in the toe of Italy. They raised cattle and the origin of their name may be a corruption of the word for 'calf' in the Oscan language, 'viteliu'. Oscan, together with Umbrian and Latin, were the main languages of the peninsula before Latin swept the others away.

The name *Itali* came to be applied to the inhabitants of southern Italy in general some time during the fourth century BC. A hundred years later the people of Central Italy were being called Italians, and by the second century BC the name referred to the inhabitants of the whole peninsula. Italia became the official name of the country by decree in 42 BC under Octavian. Three centuries later during the reign of the Emperor Diocletian the name Italia was extended to cover the islands of Sicily and Sardinia.

Then during the Middle Ages, with the development of new centres of power, in Lombardy, Venice, Florence, Naples and Sicily, each with separate identities, Italy lost its political although not its cultural connotations; so that while he may have appeared cavalier to the patriots of the new Italy, Metternich was not so far off the mark even in the mid-nineteenth century when he made his famous reference to Italy as being only 'a geographical expression'.

There is an Italian word which expresses succinctly the idea of belonging first to a town and only second to a nation, a concept that remains perhaps more important in Italy than in any other country in western Europe. The word is *campanilismo* which means literally your allegiance to your local community within hearing distance of the bells of the church tower or *campanile*. The word is usually employed in a slightly derogatory sense, particularly in reference to ambitious politicians who manage to perform miracles for their fellow townsmen by virtue of their position in central government in Rome. The case comes to mind of Senator Amintore Fanfani, four times Prime Minister, who managed to cause a bulge in the motorway between Rome and Florence which was built in the 1950s, in order to bring it nearer than originally planned to his home town, Arezzo. But there is a positive side to *campanilismo* too. It means a recognition of the sturdy qualities of pre-industrial Italy, the attachment to a local culture to which most Italians feel at least as great an allegiance as to their nation. The extraordinary popularity of soccer in Italy is one manifestation of this. Cheering on the local team, or supporting with flags and great noise one of the two local rivals in cities that boast two internationally famous teams, such as Rome, Milan or Turin, is an important and enthusiastically observed Sunday ritual for millions of Italians, cutting across all social classes and geographical divisions.

Some sporting events are of great antiquity. The gondoliers' regatta in Venice was first staged in the fourteenth century, and since being revived earlier this century attracts more than half the total population of the lagoon city, as well as a large crowd of tourists, each September. The Palio, a horse-race run with complicated rules and ritual around the town square in Siena, is the occasion for total bedlam in that usually staid Tuscan city on two summer weekends each year. The four formerly independent maritime republics, Genoa, Pisa, Venice and Amalfi stage an elaborate rowing regatta in decorated barges each year, and top the proceedings with a pageant in historical costume.

Increased mobility because of the rapid growth in car ownership, and internal migrations involving millions of families do not seem to have destroyed the Italians' innate sense of belonging first and foremost to the town where they were born.

Professor Leonetto Tintori at seventy-five looked back on a distinguished career as a restorer of fresco paintings, which has taken him to many parts of Italy and on extensive foreign travels. He was born in Tuscany and for over fifty years has lived in a house hidden among the olive trees on a hillside outside Prato. He explained to me why provincialism is a virtue, a quality, as far as he is concerned.

'When I was twenty, I used to think Prato was a pretty awful place, and that I was a citizen of the world, but now I realise just how strongly I am attached to my native town. I am proud to be a provincial in the sense that I know where my roots are – here. I have noticed that Sicilians behave like that as well, they have a great sense of belonging to their island. Bad provincialism is the incessant search for what is foreign – the acceptance of the notion that things or ideas are better simply because they come from abroad.'

Professor De Rita's researchers at CENSIS have been attempting to assess the quality of provincial life in Italy by comparing a set of positive and negative indicators in all the ninety-five provinces which make up the mainland and the two islands of Sicily and Sardinia.

They took into account such factors as the size of bank deposits, *per capita* income, the consumption of electricity, the number of telephones installed, and the availability of doctors, chemists and hospital beds, as well as the number of crimes committed, the death rate from cancer, and the suicide rate.

The results, not surprisingly, showed a huge gap between north and south. The top ten cities with Trieste in the lead were all in the north, while the bottom ten were all south of Rome. Avellino, near Naples came absolute bottom of the list. The cities where you live best in the Italy of the eighties are the smaller ones – Bologna, Florence, Ravenna and Parma – not the overcrowded metropolises of Milan (18th) Rome (35th) and Turin (51st).

But the parts of Italy where the quality of life is said to be highest are also inhabited by an ageing population. Trieste is a city of retired people, a mere shadow of its former existence as the port of the Habsburg Empire. Children's crèches are closing down and being replaced by old people's homes as the birthrate declines. Yet Palermo, where a third of the population is under the age of nineteen, holds the record for the city with the fewest sports facilities in Italy, in relation to its size.

While Italians may feel inclined to tell the small army of pollsters who tour the country what they think about every subject under the sun, they are most unwilling to tell the government how much they earn.

Italy's taxation system was until relatively recently extremely antiquated; indeed a plan to phase out tax-farming in Sicily (a system whereby the right to collect small amounts of tax is sold by the state to a contractor, an administrative practice dating back to the time of the Romans) has been frustrated by an intensive rearguard action fought by the political supporters of those who make enormous profits from the system.

The changeover to a pay-as-you-earn system was completed only during the 1970s and although in theory every Italian's tax record is now computer-listed, there has been an inexplicable delay in getting the computers to work. The wrong generation of computer was ordered initially, whether on purpose we shall never know for sure.

PAYE contributors rose from only 3.5 million in 1973 to 24.5 million in 1982, but the state is still being cheated quite appallingly by taxpayers whose annual declarations bear little relationship to their true earnings.

One newspaper report of the 1982 tax figures when they were published in 1984 ran under the headline: 'Where are the rich?' Shopkeepers, businessmen and manufacturers habitually declare incomes averaging only £3,000 to £4,000 per annum, less than manual workers. About sixty per cent of businesses claimed that they were either making no profits or running at a loss.

In an attempt to get small businesses to keep tax records legislation was passed in 1980 making it compulsory on pain of heavy fines for restaurant owners, garages, hairdressers and the like to issue receipts called 'Fiscal receipts'. But the Customs Police whose duty it is to carry out spot checks report that about seventy per cent of the establishments they visit are evading tax quite openly, and that the customers don't seem to care about the new law either.

Perhaps one reason why Italians are so unwilling to hand over their money to the State has something to do with the quality of justice in Italy.

There is no shortage of judges and court officials, in fact one magistrate calculated that they outnumber the country's full-time firemen: with more than seven thousand professional judges hearing civil and criminal cases all over the country and in the appeal courts. Italy has a judge for every eight thousand inhabitants – a world record in relation to the size of population.

For years the delays in the judicial system have been legendary. At the end of 1980 there were 1,274,000 civil cases pending and 1,465,000 criminal cases (not including cases of theft of which the authorities themselves admit ninety-five per cent go unpunished). It takes an average of eighteen months before a final verdict is reached in minor criminal cases, and two years and nine months for more serious cases. Civil cases drag on for anything from three to eight years. It is no wonder that lawyers are among the wealthiest men in Italy and that jurisprudence is still one of the favourite subjects at the universities.

Professor Rosario Nicolò, President of the Law Faculty at Rome University, referring to the 700,000 or more laws on the Statute books and the eagerness of Italian parliaments to pass new laws, commented rather tartly: 'If there were an international market in law making, our product would be considered abundant, but not competitive.'

As an example of what can happen to a complicated criminal case, look at the proceedings which resulted from the massacre at a Milan bank in December 1969, the first really bad outbreak of political terrorism in Italy. The case has gone backwards and forwards from Milan to Rome, back to Milan, down to Catanzaro in the deep south, and fifteen years on a further appeal is likely to be heard in Potenza, also in southern Italy, as far away as possible from the scene of the crime in order to discourage further acts of terrorism. There have been two completely different sets of defendants, one from the extreme right, and one from the extreme left. Former prime ministers and secret service heads have been among the small army of hundreds of witnesses who have commuted all over Italy to give evidence. Two of the accused escaped to South America. Needless to say the truth about who actually planted the bomb at the bank which killed sixteen and injured almost a hundred people has never been established.

The judiciary itself has been the target of a long series of terrorist attacks during the past decade which resulted in the murder of the Vice President of Italy's equivalent of the Supreme Court, the *Consiglio Superiore della Magistratura*, nine Public Prosecutors and three investigating magistrates, not to mention the kidnapping of three senior judges, and several woundings.

The judiciary has also been under attack from within. Politics, as usual in Italy, has been rearing its ugly head in places from which it is in theory excluded. Article 104 of Italy's post-war constitution stipulates that 'the judiciary is independent of any other power in the State' but this has not prevented a left-wing organisation calling itself 'Democratic Magistracy' from getting three out of twenty seats on the board of the *Consiglio Superiore della Magistratura* in the name of 'the hegemony of the working classes'.

In the words of Antonio Buono, a former member of this august body: 'Once upon a time a person who went to court did not have to go beyond enquiring if the judge hearing his case was good, competent and a gentleman; today you have to ask the clerk of the court, or your policeman friend, or the usher what political party the judge belongs to. Is he "independent" or is he "democratic"?

Does he take part in strikes of the judiciary or not? Is he with the bosses or with the workers?'

If I have dwelt on the quality of the administration of justice in this preliminary skirmish with the Italians and their image at home and abroad today, this is because it is a good illustration of the difficulties that Italians seem to find in acting together in unison. The libretto is more than adequate, the musical score is usually inspiring, but the conductor can never seem to get the orchestra and the cast to perform together.

It also seems important to me to remember that however significant recent changes have been in the creation and transfer of wealth, Italy has always been a very poor country. Saint Francis of Assisi is not only a very popular saint, but one of the patron saints of Italy. Italians have perfected the practice of the art of poverty as a virtue.

The worldwide headquarter of the Franciscan order lies just behind the Vatican. Fra Cristoforo, an Italian friar who works there in great monastic calm, and has time to contemplate the qualities both of his spiritual mentor and of his fellow countrymen, put it this way: 'Saint Francis was very much an Italian with all the defects and virtues of his race, the taste for beauty, singing and music. Italian literature begins with the writings of Saint Francis.

'The trouble is that we Italians think we know everything. This is psychologically beneficial, but socially disastrous.

'Italians are sensual people. They like music, food, drink, beauty, self-indulgence, but work and organisation are not serious here. There was a little bit of this in Saint Francis himself. When he lay dying, he asked one of the brothers a small indulgence, to bring him a sweet biscuit, instead of a piece of dry bread.

'You may have noticed the lack of good choral music in Rome, either in the churches, or at concerts. You see, we find it difficult to get our act together. Italy is a country where there are no choirs, only soloists.'

TWO

The Disappearing *Contadino*

> The Calabrians have a sense of fatalism. They imagine life to be like one
> of their mountain torrents which sooner or later sweeps everything away.
> 'Bend, tree, and wait for the flood to pass' is one of their sayings.
>
> Corrado Alvaro

The sudden break-up of Italy's peasant civilisation, an ancient way of life that had endured since the days of the Romans and the Greeks, has taken the Italians by surprise. Near Milan, a turreted castle in the rich agricultural plain to the south of the city has been fitted out as a Museum of Agriculture, to remind people of how life used to be for their fathers and grandfathers. Groups of schoolchildren are taken round to see the rudimentary ploughs and hoes and scythes and various wooden farm implements that were the basic tools of the land for centuries, but which suddenly became obsolete within a single generation.

Agriculture has become just another industry over much of northern Italy, with the creation of co-operatives and large mechanised farms. The former peasant who cultivated his daily needs has been replaced by a technician, usually employed in the production of a single commercial crop, be it rice, wheat, wine, or fruit. The very idea of a Museum of Agriculture would have appeared ridiculous to most Italians in the not so distant past.

The whole structure of peasant life has been interrupted by the mass exodus from the land that has taken place since the Second World War. Millions of families abandoned a way of life whose rewards were simply insufficient to sustain them. But old habits die hard. Many of those who migrated to the cities hung on to their properties and benefited from the steep rise in land values. Others became rich through building speculation. Yet others created new wealth out of loans or grants from the government's Southern Development Fund, the *Cassa per Il Mezzogiorno*. In Sardinia I have met peasant families earning cash incomes of several tens of thousands of pounds a year from a flock of a few hundred sheep whose milk is sold for cheese and whose fleeces and meat bring in more cash. The distribution of peasant wealth remains very uneven.

But the depopulation of the countryside continues. The number of Italian workers actually earning their living from the land fell from thirty per cent of the total labour force in 1960 to less than ten per cent in 1984, and is still declining.

A hundred thousand farmers from all over the country converge on Rome to demonstrate against the EEC's Common Agricultural Policy, a price support system that the Italians feel is weighted unfairly in favour of northern Europe's dairy farmers, and against the Mediterranean's growers of wine, fruit, and olive oil. One farmer stands up and puts the whole argument in a nutshell.

'When I was a boy, my father kept one cow and eight children. Now with eight cows I can't afford to keep my only child!'

On the windswept plains of the Aspromonte, the Bitter Mountain, three thousand feet up on the southern tip of Italy, Domenico Novellone manages to survive working two hundred acres that he owns scattered in several plots without hired help, but with his family. They grow and make virtually all the food that appears on their table. Domenico, aged forty-two, has a five-day week job with the local Forestry Commission, cutting trees, maintaining roads and embankments, for which he receives a cash wage of about eighty pounds a week. But as soon as he clocks off work after four in the afternoon, and every weekend, he is hoeing or planting in the fields until dusk, or looking after his cows, goats, pigs, chickens and rabbits. The Novellones not only bake their own bread and make their own pasta, cheese, wine and olive oil, but also their own soap.

Domenico told me: 'It has always been a life of sacrifice.' For his first six years of marriage he left his family behind in Calabria to work abroad on the railways. But now he prefers to be with them and to share their remote and hard life. Holidays are out of the question. His wife and five children have never travelled further afield than the neighbouring local town of Reggio Calabria, forty miles away on the coast. His eldest daughter, Vittoria, aged seventeen, is about to get married. She confided that she had never been to the cinema in her life, nor bathed in the sea, nor been alone for five minutes with her fiancé without a chaperone being present.

She spent two years collecting her trousseau, consisting of dozens of embroidered tablecloths, sheets, towels and nightdresses, enough for a lifetime, given the limited social opportunities that Calabria may appear to afford even in the prosperous 1980s.

Vittoria's future husband, Domenico, has done his military service, but like most of the young men of Calabria has no job, or prospects of one. The two families have clubbed together to buy a house for the couple near their own farms, and to furnish it.

The wedding is certainly the most important event in Vittoria's life. Over five hundred guests have been invited to the reception held in a hall down on the coast which does nothing else but cater for these mammoth family celebrations. The seven-course meal, all locally produced, the wines, the aperitifs, the orchestra, the new clothes, the photographs, and the honeymoon are likely to set the Novellone family back at least ten thousand pounds; but they are content to spend years of savings and even get into debt in order to carry out correctly the social obligations of a society which may in the eyes of outsiders be living at subsistence level, but which carries on ancient traditions with real satisfaction.

In its essentials Vittoria's wedding does not differ very much from the marriage ceremonies portrayed on a group of terracotta tablets dug up by archaeologists not far away from their home and now on display in the local museum in Reggio Calabria. The images date from the fifth century BC when this part of Italy formed part of *Magna Graecia*. You can see the bride and groom in the shape of Greek divinities walking in procession and then standing side by side to receive offerings from their guests, just like Vittoria and Domenico.

Afterwards bridal couple and guests all dance the Tarantella, a dance which can also be traced back into the mists of Mediterranean prehistory. Greek dancers with tambourines and flutes can be seen performing the fifth-century-BC version of the Tarantella in the Reggio museum. The Calabrian Tarantella can be a violent dance. It mimes a duel with its intricate steps and its rhythm can unleash uncontrollable passions. Since 1950 a local law has banned street performances of the Tarantella, which remains one of the most popular forms of entertainment at weddings and private celebrations and can go on for hours.

Just across the Straits of Messina from Calabria, on the east coast of Sicily, another long-surviving member of Italy's peasant culture, Francesco Longo, known to his family and friends as 'Piscibonu' – the Good Fisherman, in local dialect – has spent his eighty years in close contact with nature, earning his living as a fisherman.

The local fishing industry is in a state of crisis because the Mediterranean is over-fished and trawlers and factory ships from as far away as Japan now compete with the small fishing boats of Italians like Piscibonu. He is an expert in hunting the swordfish. It can attain a length of ten feet or more, and has instead of teeth a long bony snout, sharp and slender as a sword, and strong enough to pierce the hull of your boat if you are unlucky. The swordfish has been caught in the Straits of Messina since the days of Homer. The season is limited to only four months in summer as the shoals pass through the Straits on their way to their breeding grounds, criss-crossing between the Aegean and the Tyrrhenian sea.

The Greek historian Polybius described in vivid detail the harpoon kill in the first century BC.

'The beast surfaces and the boat approaches and the fisherman spears it from the prow. Then he withdraws the harpoon, leaving the barbed hook in the body of the swordfish. A long cord is tied to the hook which is let out until the fish, with convulsive movements, tires of trying to escape. Sometimes the oarsmen are wounded by the great angry fish through the side of the boat; the battle is similar to a wild boar hunt.'

The ancient Romans used to serve swordfish at banquets on dishes borne aloft by slaves wearing garlands of roses, to the accompaniment of flute music. They prized the fish as greatly as the sturgeon. Today it is still considered a delicacy and fetches a good price in the fish markets, although we have dispensed with the ceremonial. A big swordfish can fetch up to five hundred pounds.

The specially-equipped swordfishing boats or 'feluccas' are bigger and sturdier today than they were in the time of Polybius, but the method of fishing remains the same. The harpoonist stands on a long catwalk sticking out from the prow of the boat, and a look-out on top of a tall mast spots the fish from up to a mile away. The arrival of motorboats killed much of the thrill of the chase. The old wooden 'feluccas' with their tall masts can be seen rotting away in a ships' graveyard on the beach near the lighthouse at the extreme eastern point of Sicily, a stone's throw from Piscibonu's neat two-storey house which stands right by the sea.

'The swordfish is a good and faithful fish, as my late father used to say, not like the tuna which is sly and thieving and moves really fast; the swordfish moves calmly and majestically and when it knows it has to die, dies with all its heart,' Piscibonu told me. 'The swordfish is delicate and light to eat whereas you have to drain the tuna of its blood in order to eat that.

'There was a ritual my father followed when he caught a swordfish. He scratched the sign of the Cross on the cheek with his fingernails, just like we do, and then he cut a small piece and ate it raw and washed it down with a little wine. In those days there used to be plenty of fish but not nowadays. We manage to survive because we receive a pension as well, but you can't maintain a family today just by fishing. Life is too expensive.'

Piscibonu's wife Lilla looks back with satisfaction at their forty-five years of married life, but she has had her share of anxiety, too.

'I worry when the weather is bad, when it's windy or stormy. I'm always hoping the boat doesn't capsize. There have been many accidents. Three years ago Piscibonu was at sea in a storm and I was very scared. Last year, two fishermen friends of ours, brothers, were drowned at sea in a storm. It's a dangerous life,' she said.

Piscibonu and Lilla have lived all their lives almost on the very site of the dreaded Scylla and Charybdis of Greek mythology. Sailors in the Mediterranean have always feared the currents and the treacherous weather of the Straits of Messina; Homer recounts the belief of the ancient Greeks that there was a six-headed, twelve-footed monster living in a cave on the mountainside above the present-day village of Scilla on the Calabrian coast opposite Piscibonu's house, which used to devour unsuspecting navigators.

Charybdis was the fabled whirlpool, just around the headland from Piscibonu's village which, according to Homer: 'three times a day sucks the dark waters down, spews them up, and three times more swallows them down.'

Against Charybdis, Homer added comfortingly, there was no defence.

Piscibonu does not remember the devastating earthquake which destroyed his native city, Messina, at the beginning of this century as he was only three years old at the time. There was great loss of life – over sixty thousand dead – as buildings collapsed and a tidal wave swept over the survivors, washing many of them out to sea where they drowned.

But he does remember that he spent the first fifteen years of his life in a family home which was a shack constructed out of planks of wood brought by a British warship to Messina as part of an international relief effort.

'My father [he died in 1963 at the age of eighty-nine] never had a motor boat for fishing, and I didn't own my first one until the 1950s. We rowed all the time until then. It only took an hour to row to Scilla. But motors don't make all that much difference to the catch from small boats. They cost a lot to run and repairs cost a fortune.

'Before the war there was very little money about, extremely little cash. I suppose the best time in my life was when I became owner of my own house and boat when my father died. Then during the war there was the period when the Americans landed and we were smuggling things and people backwards and forwards across the Straits between Sicily and the mainland.'

I asked Piscibonu, who has no children, what he thought about young people in Italy today.

'Well, at least they all know how to read and write. I cannot read much, and can write only enough to sign for my pension, but Lilla, she can write well. Young people today call everyone by the familiar "tu". My father would have given me a good hiding for that. The children all go to school, but in my opinion there's precious little education.

'We eat fish almost every day. It used to cost practically nothing, but now it's expensive, two, three or four pounds a pound. Relatively speaking a fisherman earns much more today than in the past. Why, in our village there are even five butchers' shops today selling meat, apart from the fish market. But none of the young men want to become fishermen like me. It has become a pastime for old men. Young people today want a regular wage and time off.'

Patience is the quality Piscibonu says he admires most in his profession. ' "A hundred years and one minute" is what we used to say we needed for a good catch. You don't see anything, and then suddenly all hell breaks loose, you catch three, four, or more. The most swordfish I ever harpooned myself in one day was seven. But that's impossible now, there just aren't the fish about.'

Looking at the panoramic view over the Straits of Messina from Piscibonu's balcony, I felt I understood the intense love that this Italian expresses for his watery environment. Just along the coast on the way from Messina, I had noticed some of the names given to the fast-developing holiday suburbs along the coast. Even strangers feel the poetry with villages bearing such names as Pace, Contemplazione, and Paradiso – Peace, Contemplation and Paradise.

Piscibonu's village carries the more prosaic name of Torrefaro, which means lighthouse-tower. But the pull of the sea is something he still finds irresistible, even after a lifetime of fishing.

'The sea is a friend to me,' he said. 'I'm always drawn towards it, as if it were a woman attracting me. Yes, it's just like being in love with a woman whom I want to hold in my arms. I'm crazy about the sea. I get up from my bed at dawn and go straight to it. I have to see it as soon as I wake.

'My wife says: "If you don't take the boat out, you cannot stand it." And I say, if I have this longing, I just have to go, whatever you think. I can't help it. On summer nights, before going to bed, I go out onto the balcony, I have to gaze on my friend. The sea is better than a wife to me, I'm so fond of it. Yes, I have two wives, the water and my real wife!'

Many inhabitants in the fishing village of Torrefaro rent out their modest homes during the summer to tourists from abroad or from the hot and crowded cities of northern Italy. 'Sometimes,' Lilla told me, 'you can hardly move on the beach outside our house, there are so many people.' High rents are offered, and accepted, over a thousand pounds just for the month of August. But Piscibonu and Lilla are not renting their house to strangers. 'It wouldn't make any sense, we would not want to be anywhere else,' he said.

Two hundred and twenty-five miles from Torrefaro, on the southern coast of Sicily, opposite the shores of North Africa, is the island's main commercial fishing port, Mazara del Vallo.

About two hundred trawlers from Mazara fish the waters of the central Mediterranean, bringing in an income of over a hundred million pounds a year and some slight prosperity to a part of Europe which is otherwise in economic decline.

It is a far cry from Piscibonu's modest scale of fishing, with ten-man crews setting out for up to a month to fish red mullet, octopus, prawns, shrimps, lobster, turbot, sole, and dozens of varieties of Mediterranean fish which go to make the tasty fish soups which are enjoyed in this part of Europe.

But it's an equally hard life, and the risks are even greater. On the bustling small quayside I met former trawler captain Mario Passalaqua, a victim of a forgotten fish war fought with gunboats of the Tunisian and Libyan navies over the fishing grounds off the North African coast. Mazara is only eighty miles from the Tunisian shore. In 1978 Captain Passalaqua was fishing in Tunisian waters when shooting broke out from a patrol vessel.

'I went inside the cabin to get my permit but the firing continued. My brother was hit and died immediately. I received a bullet in the shoulder and I am still carrying around the shrapnel as the doctors said it could not be removed safely. Needless to say I never received any compensation either from the Tunisians or from the Italian government.'

The incident put an end to Mario Passalaqua's career but the 'fish war' continues, unreported and unnoticed in the rest of Europe. Up to twenty vessels from Mazara's fishing fleet are usually impounded by the Tunisians or Libyans at any one time, and the owners have to pay hundreds of thousands of pounds in fines each year to get the trawlers released. The fishing treaty between Italy and Tunisia has expired, while there never has been an official fishing agreement with the Libyans. One trawler owner told me that his vessel had been impounded by the Libyans over four years previously and he had been unable to get it back despite a finding by a court in Tripoli that it had been twenty-five miles away from the coast when intercepted and captured. The captain had spent nine months in jail and the crew three months before being sent home.

Most of the Mazara trawlers are equipped with the latest radar and sonar equipment for detecting shoals of fish, but the paint is peeling on the hulls of many of them. There is little money to spare for maintenance.

'It costs me three thousand pounds just to take this ship to sea,' Captain Franco Giacolone told me in the cramped quarters behind his wheelhouse as he prepared to set out. 'So we have to catch a minimum of three thousand pounds worth of fish just to break even. No wonder many crew members prefer to get a secure job on land, where at least you know how much money you are going to have in your pocket at the end of the month.

'No one in his right mind would encourage his children to follow him as a sea captain. In ten years time this place will be dead.'

Among Franco Giacolone's crew I noticed several Tunisians, who are increasingly replacing Sicilians as the young generation move away from Mazara or find alternative jobs.

Over three thousand Tunisians are now living in a quarter that the locals call the 'Kasbah'. The scene there is indistinguishable from that in any town on the North African coast just across the water, with Arab music blaring from the open windows. There's a keen local debate going on about whether or not this is a desirable development. The fact is that the law of supply and demand is operating and Tunisians are cheaper to employ and cost nothing in social security payments as many of them are in Italy illegally without papers.

Captain Giacolone seemed to have a low opinion of them as seamen, however. 'They are thick!' he exclaimed. 'Tunisians are no good as seamen. You tell an Italian to do something and he learns how, but not these people.

'I have been seized four times by the Tunisian navy. It's no joke. The temptation to go into Tunisian or Libyan waters is very great. There are so

Opposite Sicily: Vines and corn near Trapani, western Sicily

Sicily: Scopello, near Castellammare del Golfo, Palermo

The fishermen of Torrefaro, overlooking the Straits of Messina, find it harder each year to earn their living from the sea

Torrefaro

Torrefaro: the special boats used for harpooning swordfish have changed little in two thousand years

The Straits of Messina separate Sicily from the Italian mainland
Opposite Torrefaro. Italian houses are built to keep out the sunlight

Beach group playing cards

Left For the younger generation in Sicily, fishing is a pastime, rarely a living.
Right The Good Fisherman has no children of his own but enjoys his extended family of nieces and nephews

Opposite Francesco Longo sells his day's catch as soon as he gets back to the beach

many fish over there that they are dying of old age. Those people are no good as fishermen.'

In ancient times, when the sea abounded in fish enough for everyone (the mosaic decorations of Roman villas excavated in Sicily show as many fishing scenes as in those dug up in North Africa) the island of Sicily and the southern mainland of Italy was covered in dense forest. The productivity of the land has always been a problem since the forest cover was destroyed and the hillsides bared by erosion. The reason can perhaps be found in a story noted by an eminent historian of Italian agriculture, Emilio Sereni, who died in 1977.

Professor Sereni heard the tale from an old woodcutter in a remote village in Calabria, and it goes like this.

A peasant weighed down with a large family and poor crops sought advice from King Solomon. 'Go, my son,' Solomon said, 'you need new land and red oxen.'

So the peasant went and invested his meagre savings in a piece of land and two fine red oxen which he harnessed to his plough. But still the crops failed and he turned once again for advice to Solomon.

'Foolish man!' said Solomon, 'you did not follow my instructions. Your new piece of land has already been sown many hundreds of times, the only new land is the virgin forest. And your oxen are not red, they are brown. Only fire is red. Go to the woods and select a new piece of land each year. Plough with fire and sow your barley in the wood ash, and you will reap abundant harvests.'

Professor Sereni's etymological researches[1] indicate that continuities between Greek, Latin and modern dialect terms used in agriculture in southern Italy all suggest that for up to three thousand years the inhabitants of this part of the Mediterranean have continued to slash and burn to grow their food. This, he argues, accounts not only for the severe deforestation and erosion of the land, but also for the spreading of the maquis, the thick Mediterranean underbush, and the supplanting of the original native evergreen ilexes by more fire-resistant species of pine trees.

One tree that grows in abundance all over southern Italy is the olive, which survives drought and poor soil, although it needs careful nurturing to produce the best oil. The olive groves near Palmi in Calabria are still full of huge trees, seventy and eighty feet high, hundreds of years old, which still produce high-quality oil. Until the Russian revolution, the lamps which flickered in front of the icons of thousands of Russian churches burned Calabrian oil, which was exported all over the world.

But the flight from the land, and competition from Greece, Morocco and Tunisia has led to a crisis for Italian olive growers.

Gianfranco Filiasi, an agronomist, is president of the Olive Growers Association. 'What could we do against powerful multi-nationals like Unilever

Opposite Lilla Longo, Francesco's wife

which had to market their vegetable oils? They had the millions to advertise the fact that they are "not dangerous to the heart", or "less fat" without mentioning such important matters as the fact that fried seed oil is much more dangerous and toxic than fried olive oil.

'The British and the Germans have imposed hidden tariffs to protect their margarine and beer, at the expense of our oil and wine, and the rest has been done by our own industrialists who have preferred to make their profits by rectifying oils unfit for human consumption and mixing them to produce what they call olive oil but which has only the colour of the olive.'

'In many parts of southern Italy the olive tree is reverting to its wild state. It simply occupies the land. We spray insecticides from the air and the plant does the rest by itself.

'Our reformers have always confused the relief of poverty with the maintaining of production. They never asked themselves whether the old system of land tenure was necessary or not, they seem to have simply decided that it was the root of all evil.

'We haven't been lucky through history in these parts. First we had the Bourbons of Naples who restricted the cultivation of land to protect the revenue they received from pasturing the flocks which came down from the other side of the Abruzzi mountains. Then we had in rapid succession Fascist and Christian Democrat land reform, thousands of millions of pounds thrown away in dividing up the land into small farms with useless roads and unproductive vineyards, and plots for farmers where there was never enough water for irrigation.'

The post-war peasant revolts of southern Italy, in which agricultural workers were shot by police for demonstrating in favour of land reform, and many were thrown in jail, are not episodes that gained much attention outside Italy. But they reflected a bitter reality best remembered today perhaps in the writings of a young poet called Rocco Scotellaro, who became the youngest mayor in Italy when he was elected to lead his native village of Tricarico in the deep south in 1946 at the age of only twenty-three. He had a punctilious attitude to his job and threw himself into the peasants' struggle, getting himself arrested on a trumped-up charge of corruptly distributing food parcels. He died at the age of thirty.

The years of the 1950s are documented for us in the films of those years, the early Fellinis and De Sicas. It is surprising seeing them again, three decades later, to look at familiar urban scenes without the street clutter of today. The streets of Rome or Naples, almost devoid of cars, look as if they belong to another century. But even at this period cities were still confusing places for country people.

Rocco, visiting Naples for the first time, found it appalling and was relieved to go back home to his familiar peasant world.

1. *Terra nuova e buoi rossi* and other essays, Emilio Sereni, Einaudi, 1981.

People are only worried
About what they are selling.
Everyone makes his voice heard.
I am less than nothing
In this crowd of ragged people.
Caught up in the vortex of their own worries.
I am a man of passage, you can see
From the cloth which wraps
My mountain possessions.
The train at platform number eight
Needs many hours yet
To stir its limbs with a whistle.
I don't want to hear those screeching
Carcases of trams.
I don't want to hear any more about this city,
The frontier, where my ancestors wept
On leaving for their long voyages overseas.
I return to the den of my village,
Where we are jealous of one another.
It will be a sleepless night, waiting
For the houses to be whitened by the dawn.
And yet my home is like a birdcage
Suspended in the freedom of the sky.[2]

Rocco was a prophet. In 1952 he foresaw the failures of future governments to deal with the south.

'Land reform,' he wrote, 'does not correspond to the desires of the peasants of the south, it does not eliminate unemployment. It does not tackle the basic problems – the reform of agricultural labour contracts over the whole south, the organisation and education of the peasants . . . The political consequences will be the application of policies dictated by Rome, and the resurrection of old-type political parties based on patronage.'

In his short novel *L'Uva Puttanella*, based on his own experiences in prison, Rocco emerged as the genuine voice of peasant Italy. In the words of his friend and mentor Manlio Rossi-Doria of the University of Naples:

'He showed how the *contadini* [peasants] respect the personality of others. They know that the world is composed not only of them and the others, be they friends or enemies, but by people who have interests, problems and affections similar or dissimilar to them. The *contadini* have a view of humanity that is a good deal more balanced than that of men who grow up in urban society. Rocco broke the myth of the peasants' supposed immobility and incapacity for progress.

---

2. From Rocco Scottelaro: *E fatto giorno*, Mondadori 1954. Il primo addio a Napoli.

'He also sensed the new earthquake that was about to uproot them and knew that the new exodus from the south would be even more dramatic than that of their fathers.'

> *There was America, radiant, far away,*
> *When my father was twenty-years-old.*
> *Now where is our America?*

Four million southern Italians, the vast majority from depressed villages like Rocco's, tore up their family roots and migrated during the twenty years that followed his death.

Another prophetic figure, much concerned with the destruction of Italy's peasant culture, was a writer from the Friuli region of north-east Italy, Pier Paolo Pasolini best known outside Italy as a film maker. He was however also a poet and novelist of talent and his novel *Ragazzi di Vita (The Ragazzi)* published in 1955 put him among the select band of Italian twentieth-century writers whose work is known abroad. The book, about life among the young people of the faceless suburbs which arose around the city of Rome after the Second World War, was translated into eleven languages and even in Italy ran into many editions.

Pasolini was indignant about the loss of traditional values which occurred in Italy during the rapid social changes after the war; in a series of perceptive articles published in the Milan newspaper *Il Corriere della Sera* in the year before his death, he bitterly attacked the Christian Democrat rulers of Italy for allowing such a state of affairs to develop.

'The Italy of today has been destroyed, exactly like the Italy of 1945,' he wrote in July 1975. 'The destruction is even more serious, because we are not standing among the rubble of houses and monuments, but among the rubble of human values.

'The peasant world is finished, and any eventual return to agriculture will not re-establish the peasant's religious values. Christian Democracy is an ideological nullity, strongly influenced by the Mafia. Having lost its point of reference to the Church, Christian Democracy modelled itself upon economic power, that is to say, the new world of production – superfluous quantities of everything – which is the exact opposite of religion.

'This capitalist revolution needed men devoid of links with the past with their values of thrift. It needs men whose lives are based upon the values of consumption and pleasure.'

'A superfluity of goods,' Pasolini continued in August 1975, 'in enormous quantities was something qualitatively new in Italian history which had previously consisted of bread and misery. To have governed badly therefore signifies not to have been able to make something positive out of this abundance. On the contrary it turned into something which corrupted and destroyed, and led to the deterioration both of the environment and of the State.'

Commenting on the massive rejection of a proposal to abrogate the Divorce law in a national referendum in 1974, Pasolini explained that in his opinion neither the Vatican nor the Communist Party had understood contemporary Italy properly.

'They did not believe the Italian people were capable of such rapid evolution. The vote was not a victory for laicism, progress and democracy but simply showed that the Italian middle classes have changed radically, I should say anthropologically . . . Early industrial and peasant Italy has collapsed, no longer exists. In its place there is a vacuum probably waiting to be filled by bourgeois values claiming to be modern, tolerant, and American.

'There has been a qualitative jump marking the passage from an archaic type of culture made up of illiteracy (the people) and of a ragged sort of humanism (the middle classes) to a modern mass-culture. It is an event of enormous importance; above all, it has changed the nature of power in Italy.

'The cultural levelling process affects everyone, lower classes, bourgeoisie, workers and under-proletariat. The matrix that forms all Italians is now the same. There is no longer any appreciable difference between an Italian Fascist and an Italian anti-Fascist. They are culturally, psychologically, and what is most impressive of all, physically interchangeable. In daily behaviour, there is nothing now apart from a political meeting or a political act to distinguish a Fascist from an anti-Fascist. And as far as extremists are concerned the levelling process is even more radical.

'You can talk for hours today with a member of the bomb-throwing Fascist youth without realising what he is, whilst until only ten years ago not so much as a word, simply a glance was enough to identify him.'

Pasolini's words were borne out a few years later during the height of the terrorist wave, when it became apparent that it was difficult even for the police to distinguish between the opposite ends of the extremist political spectrum; the Red Brigades and neo-Fascist groups used the same political jargon, called themselves the same sort of names, and dressed in the same way, and used similar methods to gain their ends.

One of Pasolini's best films, *Accatone*, dealt with the problems of the underworld of the *borgate*, the suburbs of Rome, in 1961. He used ordinary young people as his actors.

In 1975 he wrote: 'Between 1961 and 1975 something basic has changed. There has been a genocide. One of those cultural genocides like the ones which preceded the physical genocides of Hitler. If I had gone away during those years, I should have had the impression that all its inhabitants had been deported or exterminated or substituted by slave workers, wild people, unhappy ghosts.

'If I wanted to make the film *Accatone* again today, I should not be able to. I should be unable to find a single young person able to repeat the same lines; they would have neither the spirit nor the mentality to speak them, and in addition they would not even understand. They would have to do the same as a Milanese lady reader in the fifties when she read *Ragazzi di Vita* – look up the words in a dictionary.

'The characters in *Accatone* were all petty thieves or people living from hand to mouth. It was a film about crime. Naturally they were surrounded by the ordinary people of the suburbs who turned a blind eye towards crime, but did normal jobs for tiny wages.

'But as a writer, and as an Italian citizen, I was not condemning those characters; all their vices seemed to me to be normal human vices, pardonable ones, and in the social context, fully justified. On the whole they were enormously *simpatico* characters. But the genocide has wiped them off the face of the earth. In their place are now some of the most odious characters in the world.

'I suppose that more than half the young people who live in the suburbs of Rome today are, from the point of view of their judicial record, honest citizens. But they are no longer *simpatico*. They are sad, neurotic, uncertain, full of lower middle class anxieties. They are ashamed to be called working class and try to imitate the sons of the middle classes.

'People who criticise my catastrophic vision of what Italy is like today pity me because they say I don't take into account the fact that the consumer society and crime are phenomena that you will find all over the capitalist world and not only in Italy.

'True, in New York or Paris or London there are dangerous criminals about as well. But there the hospitals, the schools, the old peoples' homes, the museums, the art movie houses, all work properly.

'Accatone and his friends have gone under, have met the final solution in silence, even mocking their executioners. But what are we middle-class people who are left behind doing about it?'

Twenty-four days after those words were published in Italy's biggest circulation daily newspaper, *Il Corriere della Sera*, on 2 November 1975, Pier Paolo Pasolini was found murdered, brutally battered to death, on a beach at Ostia near Rome. He was a homosexual, and had apparently been killed and robbed by a seventeen-year-old youth who was later arrested and imprisoned for the crime. He died a sacrificial victim to that same underprivileged crime-ridden society which he had identified and denounced so passionately.

The importance of his death was understood by Italy's intelligentsia. Six thousand people turned up at Pasolini's funeral and the oration was delivered by the country's best-known living writer, Alberto Moravia.

'We have lost a poet,' Moravia said, 'and poets are sacred.'

THREE

My Secretary is Rich

Uomo senza roba è una pecora senza lana.
A man without wealth is like a sheep without wool.

Florentine proverb

For centuries Italians have been trail-blazers and innovators in the world of banking, commerce and industry. Marco Polo's travels from Venice to Asia in the thirteenth century were undertaken in pursuit of trade as much as adventure, and Florentines, Lombards, and Genoese were the founders of the modern international banking system.

Business tycoons are no novelty in Italy. I visited the house of a fourteenth-century merchant who lived in the prosperous small industrial town of Prato, near Florence. He made his fortune setting up what we would now call a trans-national trading corporation. With the profits, he built himself a fine town house decorated inside and out with fresco paintings. The paintings have faded, but the building is substantially as it was when it was the home of Francesco di Marco Datini, his wife Margherita, and a large domestic staff including at least two slave girls, for among the commodities that Datini traded in – wool, skins, furs, salt, silk, dyes, spices, cotton, rice, leather, swords and ceramics – were slaves from Africa and the Levant.

What is extraordinary about Francesco di Marco Datini, apart from his success story, is the knowledge we have of his daily business transactions and his private life through the hundreds of account books and ledgers and more than 150,000 letters carefully preserved under the terms of his will after he died in 1410. They only came to light by accident just over a hundred years ago and are still being catalogued by scholars.[1]

When I picked up one of the letters in Datini's neat hand to his agent in Barcelona I saw that it was dated November 1399 and reflected that it was in considerably better shape than some of my own newspaper cuttings from only a year or two back. The caretaker of Datini's archive informed me with some pride that all the information from the letters was now being fed by scholars into a computer, and I could not help thinking that if the merchant of Prato were alive today he would surely be into computers in a big way. In the year 1399, notwithstanding war, plague, poor road communications, piracy and

1. See *The Merchant of Prato* Iris Origo, Jonathan Cape, London, 1957.

banditry, his trading house was dealing almost on a daily basis with London, Paris, Bruges, Rhodes, Alexandria and Valencia. He covered the whole Mediterranean and conducted his correspondence in ten languages, including English.

Francesco Datini, like millions of Italians in the succeeding centuries, set off abroad to seek his fortune. As a young man of sixteen he had apprenticed himself to a Tuscan merchant in the prosperous city of Avignon on the Rhône, where the presence of the Papal Court at that time afforded a steady market for luxury goods. There was a large community of Italian artists and craftsmen residing in Avignon making silver and gold ware for the tables and altars of the Pope and his Cardinals, building and decorating their palaces, weaving and stitching their fine clothes and vestments.

By 1361 he was established in business on his own account, trading in suits of armour, and even on occasion renting out coats of mail to knights unable to pay cash. He dealt in religious pictures, jewellery, fine saddlery, linen and blue cloth from Genoa (the same sort of material used for modern jeans which take their name from the Ligurian port city), painted coffers from Florence for the linen for bridal dowries, silk curtains, bath towels, and he even opened a wine tavern. But the uncertain political situation following the declaration of war upon the Pope by Florence and the Pope's retaliation – an interdict against all Florentine merchants – coupled with the return of the Papal Court from Avignon to Rome in 1378, led Francesco to return home to Prato to continue his international trading activities.

There he entered the trade upon which the small fortified town's fortunes have always been based – textiles. He imported wool from abroad – the best and most expensive came from the Cotswolds in England – gave it out to be teased, dyed, woven and cut, and then exported it again in the form of fine velvets and cloths for the nobility of all Europe. One of the letters written by his trading partner, a dyer, dated 25 April 1385, shows how little the system, and the cautious mentality of the businessmen of Prato, has changed in six centuries.

'I would see how things go before we make cloth with any more wool besides that we have already. If you are pleased with our profits, we will make as much as you please; if not, we will make no more,' wrote Niccolò, the dyer, to Francesco Datini.

Today the cloth and wool merchants of Prato set out with their pattern books to conquer not the Papal Court market, but high fashion and ready-to-wear markets in New York, Paris and London. Any weave, pattern, texture or finish can be produced to order in Prato with a minimum of fuss and delay and at a highly competitive price.

'I suppose all you really need to start out is an office and a telephone,' Loriano Bertini, a modern merchant of Prato, told me in his hi-tech offices on a new industrial estate.

Loriano has bought an apartment in New York because of his frequent stays there on business. But he still contracts out work to small craftsmen in and around Prato to keep down overheads even though he has his own textile factory as well.

The fine wool fleeces which used to arrive in bales in Prato for transformation into costly fabrics have now mostly been replaced by bales of old clothing collected and shipped to Prato from all over the world for shredding and recycling. 'If you throw away a worn pullover, or an old coat in America, it's sure to end up here sometime,' Loriano said.

In Mario Becchi's workshop a mile or two away in a village near Prato I watched long rolls of khaki coloured cloth being woven on his looms, all locally made. 'Blankets for Iraqi soldiers,' Mario shouted above the noise. 'Three hundred thousand of them.' As in Francesco Datini's time, other people's wars still provide profits for the merchants and middlemen of Prato.

There's now a State-run school for textile workers in Prato with over a thousand pupils learning not only modern design and weaving techniques, but also the uninterrupted history of Prato's contribution to European finery. It is possible to match up sample pieces of richly coloured damask, brocade or velvet from the modest school museum with the garments worn by kings, queens and noblemen of all Europe when they sat for their portraits. Look for example at the Velasquez portrait of King Philip IV of Spain, now in the National Gallery in London, which was painted in 1630; the King's fine multi-layered velvet doublet was in all probability woven in Prato. There is an almost identical sample in this textile collection. And the elegant high-buttoned satin tunic, decorated with scissor slashes, in the fashion of the day, worn by Robert Dudley, Earl of Leicester, for his portrait, painted in the previous century and now on view just around the corner in London's National Portrait Gallery, also comes straight out of a Prato pattern book.

Prato catered, and still does to a limited extent, for an up-market textile trade which had nothing to do with cottage craft weaving for popular use. The products were usually costly because real gold or silver thread or silk was used and weaving took a long time. The weavers of Prato even invented their own logo, which for centuries became a sort of international status symbol, even more widespread than the Gucci trademark of today. The symbol was the pomegranate, copied by the Italians from the East where it represented immortality and fertility. The pomegranate symbol decorated court dress, hangings and priestly vestments from the fifteenth century onwards.

Princes and priests having given way to teenagers as arbiters of fashion in our century. I turned to Giuliana Benetton, the creator with her three brothers, of one of the greatest marketing successes in the history of fashion to tell her story. Giuliana operates not from Prato, but from a village called Ponzano in the Veneto, in north-east Italy.

She is an unassuming lady in her mid-forties, with black hair tied sensibly back, and a flair for style that's not immediately apparent from her own rather puritanical dress. She looks after a family of four children, ranging from twelve to twenty-three in age, as well as putting in a full long working day at the Benetton headquarters.

'We tried from the start to direct everything towards young people – adults, but young adults from the age of sixteen to twenty-five or thirty.

'Our prices could be afforded by kids at university, and the clothes were good value. They are fashionable, colourful and practical. We've always tried to make very practical garments, simple jumpers, comfortable trousers and so on. I can wear our designs too and I am over eighteen! Everyone can wear the same. This jumper I am wearing could just as well be worn by my daughter.

'We started around 1965 making things out of very soft wools. We got on well because at that time the market was full of things made out of dry wools. Our woollens were attractive, warm, and cheap.

'I have always loved knitting. I began at school with knitting needles, then moved on to machines. Now I am most at home on the technical side. It can take a lot of machines to make one jumper. I have become highly specialised in working out how to make attractive garments at low cost. I like to make things which others don't or which cost three times more than I can produce them for. That's the thing which gives me pleasure, making things which everyone can afford.'

From the start the Benettons insisted on franchising their own shops, getting on for three thousand now, and still opening somewhere in the world at the rate of one a day.

The shops all have to be run according to the house style, but pay no royalties. Profits go to the owners. Before deciding on a location Benettons go to immense plans to find the best site, even to the extent of analysing pedestrian flow within a given city. Each shop orders its stock at the beginning of the season, by computer of course, and the Benetton factories produce the exact quantity that's needed, following the wise precepts of Francesco Datini.

Shops can reorder if they like in the middle of a season in what is called a 'flash' and goods are turned out specially for them, but no unsold goods can ever be returned.

All the factories are new and notable for their high degree of automation. There seem to be relatively few workers around and there is little industrial trouble. The reason is that while other textile industries had to make workers redundant to bring in the new technology, Benettons started off with automation and fewer staff.

Giuliana Benetton has a passion for work, she explained, which makes her demanding life worthwhile, notwithstanding the sacrifices it entails. And she is already thinking about the succession.

'My eldest girl will soon join Benetton. She has started learning about it and is already going round the company gaining experience. My husband is not involved however. It was always just the four of us, brothers and a sister, and we preferred that husband and wives should not get involved. If there had been another four people it would not have been the same. We all have our separate responsibilities, me with the design, and my brothers with sales, administration and production.'

The scale of the Benetton operation with its thirty million articles produced and sold each year and robot-controlled plants is staggering. In a computer area, a design passed by Giuliana is plotted into the computer in the smallest size. All the other sizes are worked out automatically. The operator then plays around with the various shapes to be cut out. By moving them around the computer screen he can see how to use the minimum amount of material. In the cutting room, tables stretch as far as the eye can see. Cutters scythe through as many as fifty sheets of cotton in different colours according to a computer print-out which is laid on top. A vast hangar-like room contains bale upon bale of brightly coloured materials piled to the ceiling, with forklift trucks and cranes collecting and delivering. In the woollens section machines whirr backwards and forwards noisily knitting complicated patterns. In another part are heaps of natural coloured plain jumpers which are then stuck in great vats of brightly coloured dye according to the colours of the season. It is more economical to dye a jumper after it has been made up. If there is a sudden rush, say, for yellow jumpers in Tokyo they can be quickly dyed and despatched.

If Giuliana Benetton is making her fortune by catering for the fashion tastes of the young, Giovanna Mazzocchi in Milan, Italy's second biggest city after Rome, is making hers by providing a service for Italy's most powerful consumer group, the car-owners. She publishes a highly successful monthly car magazine called *Quattroruote (Fourwheels)* which has the biggest circulation of any motoring magazine in Europe – over 600,000 copies. *Quattroruote* first appeared in 1956 when the ownership of a car was still a dream for most Italians and there were less than a million vehicles on the road. Now, with four out of five families running a car, which apart from the purchase of a house, represents one of the largest slices of family capital expenditure, the need for independent assessment of performance, dependability, fuel economy and value for money has become much greater in an increasingly consumer conscious society.

Giovanna inherited her publishing empire from her father Gianni, now seventy-eight and retired. She is in her mid-thirties, recently widowed with two young children. She has short, greying hair, dresses sensibly rather than fashionably, and still shows slight timidity with her employees after nine years in the business.

Her father started his publishing house in 1928 with an architectural magazine called *Domus*, which is now bought by the leaders of the profession in more than sixty countries as an authoritative guide to new ideas. Half the sixty thousand copies of *Domus* are sold abroad, and although most of the profits made by the publishing house now come from the motoring magazine, the architectural guide in four languages carries Italian prestige, taste and design all over the world.

'We cater for specialist markets and keep out of politics,' Giovanna told me. 'If you want to publish magazines dealing with politics or economics in Italy, it's very difficult to remain independent. You get subjected to a lot of pressure from political parties, or indirect pressure through the witholding of advertising.

'Another reason why we concentrate on specialist magazines is that when there's an economic squeeze Italians will give up reading general interest magazines before those dealing with their particular interest – such as motoring. *Quattroruote* even put on sales during the latest economic crisis because it now costs the average Italian a whole year's salary or wages to buy a medium-sized car so it is more important for him than ever to make an informed choice.'

Company headquarters for Domus Publishing, whose periodicals are also directed at people interested in knitting, travel, and flying (Giovanna's own hobby), as well as children (cartoons without sex or violence) and architects, is a brand new office complex near the ring road on the southern outskirts of Milan. The décor is expensive Italian kitsch. Large orange nudes decorate the outside of the buildings, and inside, hospital-like corridors stretch in all directions with bits of Roman columns made out of plastic dotted about. Giovanna's large office has fake Roman murals on the walls and she sits behind an enormous desk looking a little incongruous amid all the splendour. There are fruit trees in the extensive grounds, and there's also a vintage car museum started by her father.

A hundred and seventy people are employed by Giovanna, and the company turns over ten million pounds a year.

'Small businesses are what hold Italy together from a financial point of view,' she said, 'because the State is for all practical purposes bankrupt.

'If you move around northern Italy all you see are small businesses and most of them are family owned. I don't have any ambition to make my firm any bigger. I have reached the point where we can keep control and personal contact. The healthy part of Italy is composed of these small private companies.'

Giovanna studied Political Science at university, then spent a year working in West Germany for the publishers of *Stern* magazine.

'Then I joined the family firm, not really at ground level but at mid-level, and after four years got into management. I never felt trapped into having to go into the business, because at one time my father wanted to sell and it was a joint decision that I would carry it on.

'I don't consciously imitate my father, but I think I do copy his style. He has a very strong personality. He was unable to delegate. When I first took over, people were a little sceptical but I tried to learn from everybody. I was always taught not to walk around like the owner but to try and understand people.

'Eighty per cent of the present staff joined after me so I know most of them well. You must have the right people. If you have the right people, in the end the public will buy your product. You must understand each other. Your employee may be a genius, but if he's not on the same wavelength as you are, then it is difficult to work together.

'I think I am well accepted now. I mean, people will really do things for me not because I am running the company or I am my father's daughter.

'I find it very difficult to be tough. It's not in my character. But I do understand that in a small company like ours, you cannot have a personal understanding with every employee. I know almost everybody and I know their problems, but you must have a line of behaviour that is valid for everyone, you cannot keep on making compromises. Sometimes it's more difficult simply because you do know everybody. But the right hand must know what the left hand is doing.'

We had lunch in the staff canteen, all blue and white paint with marble-topped architect-designed tables and elegant chairs, as befits an organisation concerned with matters of design. Giovanna informed me that this was her idea.

'I thought that as you have to eat with the people you are working with at least the atmosphere should be a bit different and more comfortable to enable you to relax. That was my brief, to leave the walls as they were, but to create an atmosphere with a difference. It was not only a democratic choice but it's less expensive as well to make just one meal for everybody. Queueing is no problem because I just look around and talk to people whom I never see in the corridors. I think you feel the gap between management and employees much more in bigger companies than mine. Small companies are more flexible and decisions are reached more quickly. Big companies are at a disadvantage in human relations.'

One thing Giovanna made abundantly clear was that she had no time at all for politics at work. 'These days,' she said, 'it's very difficult not to enter areas where politics are important. But if you want to retain your freedom, you must have independent staff. We have virtually no union trouble as all our printing is carried out under contract and our own industrial relations are excellent.

'I am very careful when selecting staff. Apart from their education and work record I always look at their town of origin. If they come from Bergamo or Brescia you know with whom you are dealing. But I'm much more sceptical about southerners. The fact is that northern Italy is richer than the south; there's more to rob here! So the birthplace is very important.

'We had some special problems selling our magazines in Naples. There is a rule that unsold copies are reimbursed when returned, but to save transport costs we normally just accept the front cover of the magazine. In Naples they were selling copies of *Quattroruote* with the front cover ripped off for half price! Italians have this special gift for improvisation but sometimes it goes too far.'

Rosetta, Giovanna's home help and nanny for her children while she is away at work, comes from Puglia in the south. 'She really loves the children but like all southerners you feel she could walk out on you in five minutes if her honour is at stake. People from the south are much more passionate, depending upon their educational level, of course.

'From an educational point of view her influence is absolutely awful, because she gives the children everything they want. If they refuse to eat something, she cooks another dish, and then if they don't eat that, she cooks a third. I would prefer her to leave them hungry. She is too protective. But in every other way she is spontaneous, very clean, and pays attention that the children are not in danger, so I can really count on her.'

'Sofia and Susanna accept me going out to work, but they don't like me going out on Saturdays or in the evening. Sometimes they like to come to the office with me. They ride their bicycles in the grounds and that makes them happy. I think when children are very small they need you, but in the end it is not the quantity of time that you spend with them which is important but the quality of what you do with them. But I would be so nervous and furious if I spent my day shut inside the house, that I think it's better for them that I am not. I think I have found more or less the right balance.'

Giovanna used to be a keen rally driver, but then she took up flying, got her pilot's licence in 1971, and is now a member of the Board of Directors of the Aircraft Owners and Pilots Association. She took part in a round-Italy air race and has piloted her Piper Comanche as far afield as Beirut, Tenerife, and Norway.

'I have taken both the children flying with me. The elder one enjoys it but the younger one wanted to come straight down again and I had to make a quick landing! I'll have to wait a few more years to take them up again. But I have always loved flying. You feel free. It's nice to see the lights going on underneath you and the sun setting in the evening, and then when you make longer trips I like the navigation and the wireless contact and moving so fast from one country to another.'

Giovanna's new flying magazine *Volare* is already selling forty thousand copies a month. The editor is a former airline director who has a passion for private flying and has been at the controls of forty-nine different types of small aircraft. Private flying clubs are booming in Italy's new affluent society.

Still, most Italian workers cannot yet aspire to flying their own aircraft, and there are still those who do not own a car. Mauro Fiamenghi, thirty-four, has worked for sixteen years at the Alfa-Romeo car factory, in the northern suburbs of Milan, the opposite end of the city to Giovanna's company, and he cannot yet afford to purchase and run one of the superbly engineered sports cars that he helps to make, even with a thirteen per cent staff discount. His take-home pay amounts to about £90 a week. He lives in a modest fourth floor flat not far from Milan's pretentious Fascist-style central railway station, with his wife Caterina and his two sons Claudio and Cristian. The controlled rent is about £30 a month. There is only one bedroom, shared by the two boys with bunk beds. In the living-cum-dining room the family eat their meals, and watch television. At night Mauro and Caterina push back the dining table and extend the couch and the room becomes their bedroom. There is no bathroom and the Fiamenghis share a toilet on the landing with three other families. This also has to double up as a primitive sort of shower room. The light bulbs are low wattage to save money on the electricity bill. The family budget allows few luxuries beyond their one extravagance, the weekend retreat in the mountains, two hours away by train, where Mauro plans to retire in ten or twelve years time to cultivate his vines and fruit trees.

Italian social classes are often distinguished by the wattage of the light bulbs in their homes, I have observed. Giovanna's architect's dream-flat, not so many blocks away from Mauro, is bright with halogen lamps of the latest model. But I thought it was worthy of note that both workers and bosses have their home security problems in Milan of the eighties. Giovanna has an elaborate electronic and video alarm and entryphone system guarding her apartment, a precaution against possible kidnapping attempts, while Mauro deliberately has no telephone at home so no one can find his private address. He was once marked down as a potential target by one of the extremist left-wing terrorist groups which flourished in the factories during the 1970s.

Mauro is a dedicated trade unionist. He is a member of the local executive of the FLM, the Italian Metalworkers Union, an active shop-floor steward at Alfa-Romeo, and he bears an uncanny resemblance to Lech Walesa with his drooping moustache. He is plumpish, pipe-smoking, and reflective ('my friends see me as a severe person,' he told me) and comes from a devout Catholic family, eldest of seven children. He is also a keen member of the PCI, the Italian Communist Party, the largest Communist Party in Western Europe which in 1984 for the first time, in elections for the European Parliament, emerged as Italy's leading party, a whisker ahead of the ruling Christian Democrats. But he has no doubt where his ultimate loyalties lie.

'I think the worker who spends eight hours every day in the factory in the midst of the noise and thousands of people, needs time off just to be with his wife and children. I wish to grow alongside my sons.

'I was not brought up as a communist,' Mauro continued. 'My education was a Catholic one. I studied in a seminary when I left school as I felt the need to dedicate myself to something useful, and I thought I might become a priest. Then the vocation disappeared and I found myself at the age of eighteen in a factory with all my baggage of a Catholic education in the middle of an alien world, quite different from what I had imagined.

'I became a communist because I found again the Catholic sense of faith and charity among my communist comrades. When I needed something, a suggestion to help me in my work, it was usually the communist who was older than me who gave it without asking for anything in return, and without asking me to join his party. I was quite fascinated by the behaviour of these comrades. So at the age of twenty I joined the Party.

'There is no inconsistency between expecting my sons to go to Mass and my Party affiliation because I see faith as one thing and political identity as another. This tremendous ideological training I had as a boy, put to the test in the factory later on with the help of my communist comrades, means there was no pressure in making my political choices. But today, above my duties as a communist and as a trade union leader I still put my duties to my family as husband and father first.'

Mauro's workplace is a huge, sprawling industrial complex covering eighty acres half-an-hour's journey away from the centre of Milan.

Alfa-Romeo is a good example of how quickly and how recently Italian industry has changed scale.

The car company which originally concentrated on hand-made racing models and scored international successes on the circuits as far back as the 1920s was nationalised in the thirties, suffered serious war damage in the forties, and only went over to assembly line production in the fifties. Between 1950 and 1960 production shot up over fifteen times, while the number of man-hours required to make each vehicle was reduced to one ninth of the time taken by former artisan methods. By the 1980s 200,000 vehicles were being produced each year at factories near Milan and Naples, and a further joint venture with the Japanese company Nissan was under way.

But the State-owned company got into difficulties with stiff competition from the market leader in Italy, Fiat, still in private hands, and with internal problems. At one period absenteeism at the Naples factory exceeded forty per cent and the company consistently lost huge amounts of taxpayers' money. Southern workers in a northern industrial environment transplanted to Naples simply did not seem to fit, and the chairman once considered scrapping the Alfa-Sud factory altogether in view of its apparently insoluble management and productivity problems which were all compounded by interference from the local Mafia.

Giuseppe Medusa, head of industrial relations at Alfa-Romeo since 1979, put it this way. 'The advantages of large-scale production have gradually been eroded in Italy since the end of the sixties by the growth of industrial conflict and the contradictions which appeared between the productivity of a large organisational system and the quality of work.'

It is quite a contrast between Alfa-Romeo's main prestige concrete and glass management block – airport architecture without the hustle and bustle – and the huge noisy hangar where the cars take shape, and where Mauro spends his working life, one of 12,500 blue-collar employees. He is a quality controller and carries out spot checks as the cars progress along the assembly line.

The steel arrives in sheet form and is cut and stamped into shape by huge steaming machines, some totally automatic, others under human supervision. The cars are assembled by a combination of men and robots. The atmosphere is oppressive, it is kept artificially humid to keep the unpainted metal from rusting.

'I get satisfaction from my job,' Mauro said, 'because it is different every day and tests my professionalism. It is not repetitive, you have to have experience and intuition. I work back over the whole production process to locate flaws reported by dealers. Once I have discovered what's wrong, I make my suggestions, whether to the management or to the worker who did the particular job. I have to work out whether it's best to prevent the defect right at the beginning in the pressing shop, or intervene at the point where the car is being assembled and the worker is more involved.

'It calls for great tact on my part. The most delicate aspect is that the worker has to understand that by my speedy and fair intervention the car he is producing will be better and more competitive on the market, so more people will buy it and his job will be more secure. In my experience the workers do accept this.

'My position as a union representative helps me a lot. I very rarely have to make a suggestion twice. I am known from the union platform and workers accept in a dignified manner the suggestions I make.'

Mauro described to me the crisis in industrial relations in the seventies, exacerbated by attempts by terrorists groups to infiltrate the factory, which led to a complete restructuring of the assembly line process.

'Before, workers just did one repetitive job which they might continue for ten or twenty years, just like a robot. If there were twenty operations to perform to assemble the doors and locks for example, whilst before it was done by twenty workers each carrying out one operation, now with the new smaller Production Groups, the worker follows through with the car right to the end of the production line.

'The worker sees the car growing moment by moment, there's more understanding on his part. The product is better quality, and the worker himself also produces more. This agreement has given tremendous results. The worker takes the car each morning and gradually his work goes on growing and at the end of the day he sees in tangible form the results of his labours.'

Italy's trade union movement is going through a period of crisis with falling membership – partly perhaps as a result of past successes scored in improving pay, pensions, and working conditions since free unions were formed again after the fall of Fascism forty years ago. The three main union confederations have always been deeply divided along party political lines, and plant-level union organisation only came into effective being after the 'Hot Autumn' of 1969 when Factory Councils were set up to deal with collective bargaining and grievance procedures. Mauro is a leading member of Alfa-Romeo's Factory Council, elected to represent about 1,400 fellow workers in his department.

About seventy per cent of Alfa-Romeo workers belong to a union, much higher than the national average. Union membership in Italy is entirely voluntary, indeed the closed shop is against the law. Mauro believes the reason why more than half his fellow workers belong to the communist-dominated CGIL is consensus.

'Consensus is never an accident. We are aware of our own strength, but we don't want to take advantage of it. We listen to everyone's ideas and decide with all the others. If the contrasts are very great we impose our strength, but we have a united spirit. Even if we have to come to agreement by making a compromise, going one step lower, what we want is agreement with the other unions.'

Alfa-Romeo factory council meetings may look disorganised to the outsider, but Italian democracy at work is usually lacking in the structural qualities so dear to the Anglo-Saxon ordered mind. Workers and management representatives wander in and out at will; speeches go on all day and there are plenty of interruptions. Some speeches are prepared, others spontaneous. They reflect all shades of opinion from the need to negotiate and reflect, to calls for immediate industrial action. The better speakers receive applause, and attention. The bores are duly ignored and people, including those on the platform, chat, smoke or read their newspapers.

Mauro described relations between management and unions in his factory as 'mutually correct'.

'They always let us know what their intentions are, even if we do not share their views. From time to time we contest their decisions. Pressure normally begins with a ban on overtime working. Then strikes can be one hour a day, or half-an-hour on and half-an-hour off, plus demonstrations outside the factory.

'The difference between Italian and British unions is that here union membership is a spontaneous act, there is no closed shop. Everything we do which costs money, like hiring buses to go to some other city or for banners, or printing, all this comes from our own membership dues.

'Whenever a worker here goes on strike he loses cash. That's why we stagger the strikes so that as many people as possible take part. I think the Italian method is best. In Alfa-Romeo we have union membership ranging from ninety per cent on the shop floor down to only fifty per cent among the white collar workers.'

Industrial action when I visited Mauro was centred around company plans for laying off up to a third of the workforce for a year under legislation designed by the government to allow factories to carry out modernisation plans. The workers receive up to ninety per cent of their wages from a special 'standby fund' called *cassa integrazione* in Italian.

The unions, Mauro explained, suspected that the company was merely trying to reduce unsold stock – and get the government to pay, a not uncommon trick. There were fears that suspension, even under apparently generous terms, was merely a delayed sacking.

'There are cases in Milan or Turin where you can find workers who have been on "standby" for as much as six or seven years and for them it's clearly just a matter of time before they are declared redundant.

'Two years ago the Alfa-Romeo management put three thousand workers on temporary lay-off. I am sure when those workers saw their names going up it must have been a horrible moment, the first thing that comes into a man's mind is the problem of the family, the children.

'With a great deal of effort we managed to ensure that those workers all got their jobs back, but now it's starting all over again.

'I was shocked to hear of British Leyland workers voting to expel other fellow employees from their places of work. This is a thing which would never happen in Italy. We might vote for all workers having to pay a contribution or for workers to be laid-off in rotation, but to vote for one of your comrades to be made redundant, never! As membership is voluntary it would mean the end of unions here.

'On the Factory Council, I represent the workers who elect me, both union and non-union members. My strength is that I defend the interests of all. I believe my role is to defend a worker's interests whatever his personal views, party affiliations or job. I believe if a British worker were to be transplanted here he would change his mentality because I believe we encourage a correct attitude towards our fellow workers.'

Italy comes near the top of the list in the world strike league in terms of days lost in industrial disputes – four times as many as Britain, a hundred times more than Japan and a thousand times more than West Germany, according to the latest available figures.

As there are no strike funds the aim is maximum disruption with minimum loss of earnings, so a 'General Strike' in Italy should not be confused with the same event in other countries in terms of duration or effectiveness. Short, sharp strike action is the order of the day in Italy. And violence is rare. Acts of violence which might arise through picketing would be dealt with by police as breaches of the penal code, punishable by law.

'We do not tolerate violence by workers,' Mauro told me. 'When we strike we are not making a demonstration of physical force but of moral force.'

The demonstration I witnessed during a two-hour stoppage was orderly in the extreme. Over ten thousand workers marched up the road to the management block with the huge red Alfa-Romeo sign towering above them; there was singing, a few placards and speeches, but no appearance by the management. Then the march about-turned and returned to work, but Mauro appeared to think it had all been well worthwhile.

'The question here is to save the factory,' he said. 'The union doesn't want to save an empty factory manned by 1,500 robots, we want a factory with ten to fifteen thousand workers.

'There have been times when the management took advantage of us. They sometimes force us into difficult positions in the power game. But there are other moments when we hold the whip hand. Here at Alfa-Romeo the management has tried to find new ways to make cars and to reach some kind of relationship with the worker.

'Today, while other factories around us are closing, there is a search here for agreement which does allow us not to break off relations with the management. I believe Alfa-Romeo will survive.'

Mauro does not believe that the black days of factory terrorism in the 1970s will return either.

'The critical years were when we started the new Production Groups which gave much greater worker-satisfaction. The terrorists were against this because it stopped the fragmentation of work. Previously they were able to bring production to a complete halt by getting only three or four workers on the assembly line to down tools.

'I don't believe that the Red Brigades terrorists were ever motivated by a real ideology. They simply wanted an operational base in the factories – which in the end they did not get.'

Every weekend Mauro switches off from the problems of factory life to enjoy his rural life in the foothills of the snowy Alps. His retreat is a modest dwelling by the roadside in the village of Cino, population six hundred, the birthplace of his wife Caterina.

'I like it best in autumn when everybody comes back for the wine harvest, and the village has a different sort of intimacy as all the families get together. In winter it is beautiful as well with the snow. The people are kind and I like the narrow streets, and the simplicity and the easy-going ways. It's a bit like being in Tibet – a village outside the world, which solves its problems in a quite different way from any other small town or city in Italy.'

Cino is populated during the week mainly by women and children as most of the men are away at work in Switzerland, across the nearby frontier.

'The women work in the fields and vineyards, look after the animals, as well as their families, and life is quiet. I live in a frenetic way during the week and come to Cino for a bit of peace and quiet at the weekend, but of course the village becomes livelier on Saturdays and Sundays as the men return. They are two different worlds, theirs and mine.

'The women like to meet at the public wash-house, an old building which the authorities wanted to demolish at one time. Even though there are washing machines now, the women like to be together to discuss their problems, when the children have gone off to school and the men to work. That I think is really characteristic of mountain people.

'The children enjoy themselves, Cristian with his moped and Claudio with his walks in the woods with his friends. For the family this is where we have the togetherness we perhaps don't have in Milan. After I have been up here a fortnight though, I miss my work, but when I am back again in the factory I talk a lot about Cino to my workmates. They see how calm I am when I come into work on Monday mornings. Weekend life is very important.'

Northern and southern attitudes to work are both conditioned by the attachment to the soil of a former peasant workforce, but at the Alfa-Romeo factory near Naples, a real cathedral in the desert, in industrial terms, you feel this much more strongly. The idea of bringing industry south rather than forcing southerners to migrate north in search of a job was good in theory, but has proved difficult in practice.

Gianni Blasi, a psychologist at Naples University, told me he had seen many examples of family relationships breaking up as sons took jobs as wage-earners at Alfa-Sud. The sudden implantation of a modern factory in a peasant society at the beginning of the seventies set up strong social stresses, and also created immense problems for a predominantly northern management dealing with a workforce which until the factory was built had no concept of modern industrial disciplines.

A particularly bad outbreak of absenteeism occurred in 1980 when local doctors wrote out medical certificates for about half the workforce, enabling them to take three days off at the Italian taxpayers' expense. The unions agreed to the sacking of one hundred of the most persistent malingerers and matters improved. But sitting in the works canteen, described in a recent issue of the company's house magazine by a well known food critic as 'a real restaurant' where he found better cooking than in many establishments charging £8 for a meal, I could not help wondering just how far State capitalism can continue in Italy along its present path. Alfa-Romeo workers in Naples, as in Milan, have a staff restaurant where they pay a token one penny for their meal and three pence for any wine or beer they drink with it. And while not awarding any gastronomic stars, I could not but agree with the critic that the food was wholesome and appetising, and, by northern European factory standards, extraordinary.

Mario Nervegna runs five factories in and around Naples producing high-quality pasta mainly for sale in the discriminating and wealthier markets of the northern cities of Italy. He refuses to export his product as he says non-Italians don't know how to cook it properly and appreciate its qualities.

The story of the pasta industry in Italy since World War Two is that there has been a steady contraction in the number of firms, from about 2,500 in 1945 to a tenth that number today. A decline in consumption and a battle for markets by the big food manufacturers is the cause. However Mario Nervegna's company is doing well, using as much automation as he dares in a product that is advertised as 'artisan-made' rather than mass-produced.

But Mario complained that he too has his staff problems.

'It is almost impossible to find a good office secretary in Naples,' he said. 'There's no opportunity for local girls to get the sort of training they would have in firms in northern Italy,' he went on. 'But I am lucky. My secretary is rich!'

I asked him to explain.

'Oh, it's quite simple, she comes from a wealthy family, has her own car, is used to travel about Italy and even abroad, and knows how to use railway and airline timetables, to use her own initiative in fixing appointments and dealing with clients. Yes, the best qualification for a secretary in Naples is that she should be rich!'

FOUR

Gardenias for Immacolata

Allu carciaru ed alla ghiesia tutti ci avimu' na petra.
Prisons and churches are open to everyone.

Calabrian proverb

Giovanna Mazzocchi does not at first sight seem the type of woman to carry a gun. But she often has a pistol hidden away in her handbag.

'I take it when I go out at night alone,' she said, 'just as a precaution. I hope I never have to use it. You never know what sort of situation you might find yourself in.'

Wealthy Italians frequently employ full-time bodyguards. But Giovanna is ready to look after herself if the chips are down. The reason for her preparedness is simple. Her elder sister Maria Grazia was kidnapped in Milan by bandits in 1978 and held for ransom for sixty-five days in conditions of extreme cruelty. She was kept blindfold and chained to a bed to prevent her escaping or recognising her captors. The ransom paid for her release represented a very large sum—the family have never revealed exactly how much, but it ate up more than a year's business profits. Maria Grazia herself was traumatised by the experience and even today cannot bring herself to talk about it.

The first thing that Giovanna knew about her sister's kidnap was a telephone call at three o'clock in the morning of 25 May 1978. 'The kidnappers simply asked me if I was Giovanna Mazzocchi, and when I said yes, they told me to go to my sister's house as she had been taken hostage.

'I didn't believe it at first, so I rang up and the maid answered and she checked my sister's room and found she was not there. I went round to her flat and there outside was my sister's car, a small Opel Kadett with the ignition keys still inside, and also her shoes, indicating there had been a struggle.

'It was a professional gang. They had followed my sister's movements for months, and waited three nights in her garage before they actually kidnapped her. Her husband was away on business in America at the time, and she returned home alone after dining with friends.'

The next day the kidnap was duly reported on an inside page of the *Corriere della Sera*. There had been so many kidnaps in Milan in recent months that it no longer made front page news. PUBLISHER MAZZOCCHI'S DAUGHTER KIDNAPPED OUTSIDE HER HOUSE, ran the headline, and underneath: BANDITS DEMAND MILLION POUND RANSOM. The newspaper also published a denial by the local parish priest that he had offered to act as go-between in ransom negotiations.

The go-between finally chosen was one of Maria Grazia's schoolfriends. There was a long drawn-out exchange of messages with the kidnap gang, involving rendezvous fixed through scraps of paper left in telephone boxes, and advertisements in code in the local press. The messages from the kidnappers were always written by the victim herself in her own handwriting to prove she was still alive.

'We never had the chance to speak directly to the kidnappers, and sometimes it was difficult to understand exactly what their demands were. We were very scared that we would never see her alive again,' Giovanna said.

'After a sort of treasure hunt, involving a chase of hundreds of miles around Milan and frequent changes of cars to throw off the scent any police who might be monitoring the movements of the go-between, the agreed ransom was finally handed over in banknotes at nine o'clock one evening and by three the following morning Maria Grazia was freed.

'Coming to terms with violence in our own lives was emotionally very hard. It was the first time in my life that I had had to manage a situation over which I had no control at all. So I suppose I learned from that. I also learned that you have hidden reserves of strength. I remember a brother of a schoolfriend of mine was kidnapped about a year before my sister, and I thought at the time, my God, if it ever happened to us I should die! But I didn't. You get over it.

'What was frightening was to realise that the criminals had done their research so carefully. They knew everything about us, life, death, and miracles! It was such a total act of violence which interrupted the whole rhythm of life. Everything else lost its importance during those sixty-five days. When Maria Grazia was finally freed it took us all more than a month to recover from the strain. Afterwards there was a strange emptiness.

'I don't seriously believe we could be victims again. If you worry all the time, you would never go anywhere or do anything. But I do take precautions all the same. It must not become an obsession, as it would affect the children, so in this sense my life has not changed and will not change in the future.'

According to the Italian Interior Ministry almost five hundred Italians were kidnapped for ransom between 1974 and 1984. Most of the crimes were carried out in the rich north, and most of the bandits came from the poor south, particularly the island of Sardinia, and the region of Calabria. The millionaire victims included members of such well known families as the Agnellis, the owners of Fiat, Italy's biggest private industry, and three members of the Bulgari jewellery family, one of whom had his ear amputated by his captors.

Twenty victims were murdered by the kidnappers, either because the police were hot on the trail of the gang, or because the required ransom was not forthcoming. Some victims suffered physical mutilation, others permanent psychological damage, and most took a long time to recover from their experiences after living for months on end in a tent in the rugged mountains of the Aspromonte in Calabria, or cramped in the dark in cellars or specially-constructed underground 'prisons'. Ransoms paid varied from a few thousand pounds, to several of over five million, and the kidnap gangs showed an uncanny ability to choose victims from families whose wealth had been hidden from the taxman but none the less had the ability to pay.

A considerable number of kidnaps never come to the attention of the police as the victims' families prefer a quick private deal in order to avoid publicity in exchange for a smaller ransom. The official figures therefore just represent the tip of an iceberg, the most notorious cases.

Ferdinando Pomarici, a former Assistant Prosecutor in Milan, tried to beat the kidnap gangs by freezing the bank accounts of the victims' families to prevent them paying out a ransom. In five cases he succeeded and the hostages returned home safely without any money changing hands. But pressure to pay out when it has become a matter of life or death for the victim is often impossible for the authorities to resist. In the case of the kidnap of Maria Grazia Mazzocchi the investigating magistrate at first froze her father's assets, but then there was a change of mind and a hefty ransom was finally paid over.

The police have improved their detection techniques for kidnap crime since the worst year, 1977, when there were no less than seventy-five major kidnaps reported. Two assistant prosecutors now work full-time in Milan on kidnap cases and a special anti-kidnap centre has been set up with sophisticated listening devices for recording and tracing up to two hundred telephone calls simultaneously. A computer memorises all the details of past kidnaps including the voices, inflections, mannerisms and dialects of the 'telephonists' that maintain contact with the victims' families. New laws have been brought in to increase prison sentences for those convicted of kidnap crime, and to grant leniency for 'repentant' kidnappers who inform on their former comrades. But Carmen Manfredda, one of the two full-time anti-kidnap prosecutors in Milan, admitted: 'There are fewer kidnaps, but we are still far from hoping to defeat this very serious phenomenon in Italy as a whole.'

One worrying development is the increasing number of child victims. A seventeen-month-old baby girl, Elena Luisi, was kidnapped from her home in Tuscany in 1983. She was freed by police from an isolated farmhouse in Sicily, many hundreds of miles away, without a ransom being paid, and the gang who organised and carried out the crime were brought to justice with reasonable speed, as they had been caught red-handed. Lucio Bardi, the other Assistant Prosecutor in Milan concerned with kidnap crime, said: 'Child kidnappings could be the gangs' new order of the day. Children will never be able to recognise the voices and faces of their captors. They will never be able to give evidence in court.'

A British family from London, Rolf Schild, his wife Daphne and fifteen-year-old daughter Annabel, were taken hostage on the island of Sardinia in 1979 by a local kidnap gang. The two women were held captive first in a village, then in a cave in the mountains, for almost seven months until a ransom of several hundred thousand pounds was paid. The Schilds clearly had no idea when they bought a seaside holiday home on the northern coast of the Mediterranean island that they might fall victim to an ancient form of pastoral crime which had its origin in cattle and sheep stealing.

According to the code of Sardinian shepherds the boundaries between the theft of an animal and the capture of a human being, particularly a stranger to the island, are somewhat blurred. During the course of the kidnapping and the criminal trial that followed I had the opportunity to observe at close hand the reactions to this dramatic situation of three very different groups of people, the family themselves, the police and judicial authorities, most of whom come from the Italian mainland, and the Sardinians of the small villages in the rugged mountains of the centre of the island. This is real bandit country where the tombstones in the village cemeteries tell a continuing tale of death through violence and vendetta.

It is not so very difficult to meet a bandit in Sardinia. The word *bandito* simply means someone who has got on the wrong side of the law, and in the ancient and often primitive society of Sardinia law-breaking is so commonplace that practically every family you meet seems to have a relative who has served time in jail for crimes ranging from sheep stealing all the way to murder. The local code of justice demands absolute silence before the police and the judges. Sardinians prefer to spend long years in prison rather than to betray their friends. And no one ever admits guilt. I met one old man in the notorious bandit village of Orgosolo who had spent thirty-three years of his life in prison for a murder he still insists he never committed. His only offence, he told me, was sheep stealing.

A parallel system of justice operates in the isolated villages. The village elders give their verdicts in impromptu courts 'under the oak tree', as they say, and for the sheep farmers of central Sardinia that is the justice that really matters.

The Sardinians have a saying *'furat chie furat in domo'* which means that a robber can only be considered such if he robs at home, in other words, he who robs a stranger is not guilty of theft. Antonio Pigliaru, a local expert who has carried out extensive research into the unwritten laws of the Barbagia mountains, points out that in general the theft of cattle or sheep is not considered an offence. An offence is 'an act consciously foreseen and willed in order to damage another person's honour and dignity'. The law is viewed subjectively, so that offences which would be punishable by vendetta are, for example, the theft of the goat which provides a family's daily milk supply, or the pig being fattened for their table, or pasturing sheep on another person's land 'for reasons of provocation'.

I found in Sardinia a deep rift between the ordinary people and their government, which is organised entirely from the mainland. Italian judges, administrators and police sent to serve on the island seem to regard their period of service as a time of exile. From time to time the authorities in Rome, only half an hour away by air, get exasperated and set up commissions of enquiry or send in the army to deal with particularly serious outbreaks of banditry. The mountainous terrain, the sparseness of the population, and the lack of roads combine to defeat all attempts to dominate this ancient society. Even the Romans of antiquity failed to make much of an impression. One can understand the often repeated assessment of those sent from Rome to bring the islanders to order that the only way to deal with the situation is a 'scorched earth' policy.

Among Sardinians a sense of injustice runs deep. I heard shrieks of desperation and imprecations against the judges from the public in the Assize court at Nuoro when six local shepherds were sentenced to a total of sixty-three years' imprisonment for the attempted murder of a policeman. I saw the shepherds, handcuffed and chained together, led away from the metal cage where they had followed the court proceedings in sullen silence.

One of those sentenced was a shepherd boy of seventeen who had taken shelter with a suspected kidnap gang on the night of a gun-battle with police which led to the rounding up of the gang. This boy had a tragic personal history. His father had murdered his mother and later committed suicide in jail. His relations had clubbed together to buy him a few sheep and it appeared from the evidence given in court that he had been rounded up in error. But now he was doomed, with a criminal record of his own, and the prospect of further prison sentences hung over him. He would never open his mouth to the authorities.

I spoke with the police officer who had captured this group of shepherds. He had shot two of them dead in the darkness; luckily for him they both turned out to have long criminal records. At least a dozen times a year the police battle it out with bandits in the craggy countryside.

Driving across the almost deserted roads of Sardinia – which is considerably larger than its neighbour Corsica – it was easy to understand why the police had so little chance of discovering the hiding places where the two Schild women from London were held while the ransom for their release was negotiated. Just as in the rugged Aspromonte mountains of Calabria, another favourite hiding place for kidnap victims, there are hundreds of grottoes, and everywhere thick undergrowth, the maquis, which provides perfect cover. And any shepherd who happens to stumble upon a hide-out by accident knows that according to the unwritten code of local law, the price of betrayal is certain vendetta and death.

Most Sardinian shepherds are today far in advance of their forbears in economic terms. They travel by car, no longer on horseback or mule, but the basics of their Spartan existence have not changed significantly. Entire periods of European history have bypassed the highlands of central Sardinia. Few of the holiday visitors who now swarm around the coast of the island every summer to enjoy the sea and the sun have any concept of the lives of the Italians who live in the hidden world of the Barbargia.

The gang which kidnapped the Schild family were finally arrested and put on trial in Cagliari, the island capital, together with over fifty other Sardinians who were accused of carrying out a whole series of kidnaps of wealthy holidaymakers and residents. I sat in the courtroom as a group of the accused were formally identified by Daphne Schild as the guards who had held her and her daughter captive for months, in conditions of extreme discomfort and brutality.

After they had been found guilty and sentenced to long terms of imprisonment, some to life, Daphne Schild told me that she felt no fear at seeing these criminals again. 'I felt I would like to talk to them again, to hear of their reactions since being captured themselves,' she said. A curious relationship sometimes builds up between kidnap guard and victim, during weeks of enforced proximity.

Gaby Maerth, a pretty nineteen-year-old girl whose family lives in a splendid villa on Lake Como, was kidnapped outside her home in 1982 and spent 147 days chained to a wall in a darkened cellar in a mountain hut in the foothills of the Alps. During her captivity she and her gaoler, forty-two-year-old Roberto Piccapietra, became lovers.

'I clung to him as he represented my only hope of release,' Gaby explained after she was freed and the ransom demand had been reduced from three million pounds to less than a hundred thousand pounds when the kidnappers realised they had made a mistake in assessing her father's ability to pay.

The investigating magistrate struck out a charge of rape when Gaby admitted that she gave her full consent to the relationship. Piccapietra was later sentenced to fifteen years' gaol for his part in the kidnap. It was his weakness in falling in love with the victim that led to the arrest of the whole gang. He bought a cake for Gaby at the local village near where she was kept prisoner and failed to notice that it had the name of the village printed on the box. Gaby remembered and told the police when she was freed and this simple clue led them straight to the gang.

If there is reason for cautious optimism that the fight by the authorities, at least on the mainland, against kidnap crime is finally beginning to show results, there is less reason to believe that the battle against another well-established form of Italian criminal organisation, the Mafia, is finally being won.

The Mafia has its origins on the island of Sicily. The word first appeared in its current pejorative meaning during the nineteenth century. The term 'mafioso' originally meant 'a person of courage'. A hundred and fifty years ago a public prosecutor in Trapani, western Sicily defined the Mafia as 'a brotherhood of crime'.

'In many villages,' he said, 'there are brotherhoods whose only link is dependence upon a boss. A common fund is there when needed to clear an official from blame, to protect him, or to put the blame upon an innocent person. Many high ranking magistrates cover these brotherhoods with a cloak of respectability.

'It is impossible,' the official wearily complained, 'to get the police to patrol the streets properly or to find witnesses to crimes committed in broad daylight.'

The Mafia has shown immense flexibility in adapting itself to changing economic and social circumstances. The reason why the Mafia is alive and well and apparently flourishing all over Italy today appears to be an attitude at the highest levels of local and national government of 'tolerance bordering on connivance'. The words are those of a parliamentary commission of enquiry that sat for fifteen years sifting the evidence it had gathered and then wound itself up lamely in 1972. The commission concluded that the new Mafia, whose profits are based on the international drug trade, among other lucrative activities, 'is characterised by the search for ever greater profits in all sectors permeable to its penetration, by the daring of its projects, by the terroristic and professional nature of its violent methods, by the open challenge to the powers of the State and to public opinion, by its links with other criminal groups in Italy and abroad, and by the dangerous territorial extension of its ramifications'.

The powers of intimidation of the Mafia remain undiminished in the eighties. Its most spectacular act was the elimination of the senior police officer General Carlo Alberto Dalla Chiesa and his wife in September 1982. General Dalla Chiesa had been sent to Sicily by the government in Rome after a long and successful career in the paramilitary police, the Carabinieri, culminating in the virtual defeat of the Red Brigades terrorist organisation in northern Italy. His new mission was to clean up Mafia crime. After five months he returned to the mainland in a coffin.

Among more than a thousand Mafia murder victims, some of whose bodies were never found, in the Palermo area between 1975 and 1984, were Colonel Giuseppe Russo, the retired head of the Carabinieri's special investigation branch who had sent dozens of Mafia criminals to prison, Boris Giuliano, head of the Palermo Flying Squad, Cesare Terranova, a judge and former member of the parliamentary commission of enquiry, Piersanti Mattarella, the President of Sicily's regional government, Gaetano Costa, chief Public Prosecutor, and Pio La Torre, head of the Communist Party in Sicily.

Journalists who specialise in the Mafia do not escape either. Mauro de Mauro, a well known local investigative writer, was kidnapped and killed. His body was never recovered and the official investigation into his murder has now been officially 'closed'. Giuseppe Fava, a writer from Catania, was ambushed and killed in the street one night in 1983.

No witnesses came forward to help police into their enquiries into any of these crimes. There is a Sicilian folk-tale which expresses this concept of *omertà*, the law of silence imposed by the Mafia, which has its origin in the sense of self-preservation of a poor people in a world which they perceive only in hostile terms.

Eating and Talking, who share the same home, with the Mouth, have a quarrel. So they seek advice from a wise man on how they are to live together. The wise man says: 'Talking is for the Mouth of the rich because they already have enough to eat, while Eating is for the Mouth of the poor because the less they say, the better it is for them.'

The small agricultural town of Alcamo is perched on the sun-scorched hills behind Palermo and for years has been the centre of feuds and vendettas between different Mafia clans which spill over into local politics. In 1980 Salvatore Bennati was elected mayor on a Christian Democrat party ticket. Two days after the election he resigned on the grounds of 'nervous exhaustion'. Four years later another Christian Democrat, Baldassare Renda, suddenly resigned 'for health reasons' only hours after being elected mayor. Questions were tabled in the regional parliament about this 'brazen and arrogant presence of the Mafia in political life in Sicily'.

A new mayor was sworn in. He is a police officer, and clearly a man of courage. His name is Giacomo Grillo, and history will relate how he makes out during his term of office. In the meantime none of his fellow councillors is willing to take on the job of housing officer, because of the Mafia's well known links with the building trade. For the moment, the new mayor said he would do the job himself.

In the small Calabrian town of Gioiosa Ionica in November 1976 there was a gunfight between police and a Mafia boss called Vincenzo Ursini, in which the local Mafia leader was killed.

Word went round that as a sign of mourning the whole town was to close down on the Sunday following the killing, the day of the funeral, and that the weekly market was to be cancelled. The instructions were followed. One shopkeeper, Rocco Gatto, refused to obey. Several months later he was ambushed and murdered on a road just outside the town. No one was ever arrested for the crime.

The technique being used by the government to combat Mafia crime today centres on investigations into the assets and bank accounts of suspected bosses. A data bank has been brought into use for the first time, but those responsible for bringing these criminals to justice are aware that they are ill equipped to battle against methods of intimidation that have stood the test of many generations. The four judges dealing with Mafia crime at its hub, Palermo, have also to deal with all sorts of petty offences in the course of their official duties, and have received no specialised training in banking to enable them better to follow the labyrinthine methods now in use to recycle the profits of the drug trade into legitimate businesses. 'We are the artisans and they are the professionals' was the comment of one of these judges, Paolo Borsellini.

Public awareness in Italy of the growth of the tentacles of the Mafia all over the country has been increased by greater attention by the media, including television. One of Italy's best known film directors, Damiano Damiani, produced a six-part blockbuster drama series on the Mafia called *La piovra (The Octopus)* which was broadcast during prime time on the main RAI TV network in the spring of 1984. The critics hailed the series as a refreshing change from the cultural colonisation of *Dallas* and *Dynasty* for it dealt with a reality that is all too often swept under the carpet by those who control the programmes seen by Italy's television addicts. Two-thirds of Italy's total television audience were glued to their screens for the last episode of *La piovra*, according to a reliable audience research report.

'*La piovra* is the story of a policeman whose illusions about defeating the Mafia have been shattered,' Damiano said. 'He knows you can find corruption and betrayal even inside government, and that it is risky and often unprofitable to confront the authorities. In the end he is forced to dissimulate even though he is on the side of justice.

'Action by such a person in the current situation can only end in defeat because it seems clear to me that everyone now understands, thanks to television, the newspapers and the cinema, that at a certain level organised crime is not just a matter for police action.

'Operations to change society cannot be entrusted to the flying squad. The real cancer on the face of Italian society is not Mafia organisation, but the widespread Mafia mentality of the people. In Palermo, for example, I don't think anyone is going to name a street after General Dalla Chiesa, and in Catania, no one is going to name a street after Giuseppe Fava.

'The Mafia is not only a criminal organisation, but the fruit of a special mentality and behaviour. The Mafia has become part and parcel of the way Italians think, particularly in that part of Italy which used to belong to the Kingdom of the two Sicilies.'

In 1967 Damiani made a film version of the novel about the Mafia by the Sicilian writer Leonardo Sciascia, *Il giorno della civetta (The Day of the Owl)*.

'In those days,' he said, 'the Mafia was still bound up with a feudal agricultural economy. It enforced the respect of a certain unwritten law and fed on extortion like a parasite.

'Today it is an organisation at the service of huge illegal financial holding companies which deal in any form of criminal trading from drugs, to arms and kidnaps. The Mafia – and this is not a deliberate paradox – runs the legal side of illegality.

'It is an organisation which guarantees the keeping of agreements, the making of payments, and fair treatment for all the contracting parties. The strength of the Sicilian Mafia lies in this service which leaves colossal sums in Sicily each year – ten thousand million pounds and perhaps more. The other task of the Mafia is to launder this dirty money, to channel it into legitimate activities, such as the construction industry.'

At the end of the last episode of *La piovra* fact was supposed to take over from fiction in the form of a studio debate. Taking part were the widow of Boris Giuliano, the former head of Palermo's flying squad murdered by the Mafia in July 1979, the deputy director of the Bank of Sicily, and a leading criminal lawyer, whose clients include some big names under investigation for alleged Mafia activities.

The 'debate' was smothered under a succession of half-truths, denials and justifications which left the late-night viewer no nearer to the heart of the truth about the seriousness of the challenge to the legally constituted authority of the Italian State. The banker failed to provide any explanation of how the Mafia millions get recycled through the dozens of brand new banks which have sprung up in towns and villages all over Sicily within the last few years. The lawyer, filmed together with his banker friend in the plush surroundings of Palermo's most exclusive men's club, did an efficient whitewash job on his colleagues.

The Mafia, in its new form, has become a financial multinational with associates in the United States, Latin America, and several European countries. It produces investments and dividends and offers work and prosperity not only to its shareholders, but also to a small army of Italian businessmen, shopkeepers and manual workers, some of whom might be surprised to find out that they were actually making their living out of the profits of crime.

Professor Luigi Lombardi Satriani, an anthropologist who was born and lives in Calabria, and has taught for many years in southern Italian universities, believes that this vision of the Mafia is distorted by stereotype attitudes. 'How do we account for the persistence of the Mafia if it is simply a criminal phenomenon?' he asked.

'The Mafia only resorts to killing as a last resort. Murder is in fact a sign of weakness. The Mafia does not need publicity. And those who portray the Mafia as not being supported by the people of the south simply display their lack of knowledge.

'The traditional Mafia has a lot in common with popular folklore in the south. The values that it prizes are individual courage, a sense of honour, the necessity of vendetta to avenge dishonour, respect for your word, virility, family ties,

64   *Opposite* Milan: The *Duomo* or Cathedral. The 'Gothic' spires were added later

Mantua, Lombardy – a town famous for its palaces

Mauro Fiamenghi has worked as a quality controller at Alfa-Romeo, near Milan, for sixteen years. Mauro takes home a much smaller pay-packet than his British counterpart at BL and he takes his trade union activities very seriously. For relaxation he and his family spend each weekend at his retreat in the mountains – his wife's childhood home

Giovanna Mazzocchi is managing director of a publishing empire created by her father. She publishes Italy's leading car magazine *Quattroruote (Fourwheels)* as well as the prestigious international architectural monthly *Domus*

Left Montemilone is a village in Basilicata, an area depopulated by migration; the town has lost half its population since 1970. Seventy per cent of its inhabitants are old people
Right Dino Labriola, the Communist mayor since 1979, commissioned this mural depicting poor southern peasants from local artist Giovanni Brenna (*opposite*)

Montemilone. Time is one commodity that is not scarce in the poor south of Italy where heavy unemployment is endemic

POLIPI ALL'INSALATA
ANTIPASTI DI MARE
TARALLI CON MANDORLE E PEPE

blood relationship and *omertà*. I have studied the Mafia in many of its guises, and cannot help concluding that the modern Mafia still has something very archaic about it.'

Southern Italy's biggest city, which beats even Palermo in its annual number of murders and high crime rate, is Naples. There the Mafia is known under a different name, the Camorra, but the criminal aims and methods remain very much the same. The Camorra also traces its origins back to the nineteenth century and beyond.

The Camorra underwent a profound transformation in the early 1960s with the closing of the free port of Tangiers in Morocco, the headquarters of the Mediterranean cigarette smuggling trade. Mafia families from Sicily joined with Neapolitan traffickers to form a new organisation for smuggling cigarettes into Italy, an activity traditionally controlled from Naples.

It is estimated that at least 20,000 tons of contraband cigarettes enter Italy each year, from which the state loses hundreds of millions of pounds in revenue. But this contraband trade gives employment to thousands in Naples, where the number of jobless has always been high and it's a commonplace saying that 300,000 people go to bed each night without knowing where their next meal will come from. The cigarettes are unloaded in international waters onto power boats which bring them ashore at night for distribution not only in Naples but all over the country.

The New Camorra however has expanded its activities into other more lucrative fields, such as drugs, arms smuggling and the systematic hijacking and robbery of the huge container lorries which ply Italy's motorway network.

Undisputed king of the New Camorra is forty-three-year-old Raffaele Cutolo, who has spent most of his adult life in jail for crimes of murder and extortion, but still apparently manages to run his vast criminal empire from behind his cell door. Raffaele, known deferentially to his associates as 'the Doctor' or 'the Professor', was brought up on the streets of Naples and quickly became boss of his neighbourhood gang. He was condemned to life imprisonment for his first murder at the age of twenty-one, but with the help of complacent judges, skilled lawyers, and periods on the run, managed to get himself declared of unsound mind and was transferred for a time to a home for the criminally insane whence, of course, he managed to escape.

Raffaele regards himself as something of a genius and dismisses all talk about insanity as the febrile invention of lawyers. 'If I had gone into the Church,' he once said, 'I should have become Pope.' He named his son Roberto, after his hero Robin Hood. He dresses expensively and always looks immaculate when he appears in court, with silk shirt and Dior tie, well-cut suit and crocodile-skin shoes; his latest exploit on 26 May 1983 was to get permission to marry in the island prison fortress of Asinara, in Sardinia, where he was transferred after he

Opposite Naples: A typical Santa Lucia seafood restaurant. Despite heavy marine pollution in the bay of Naples, mussel consumption is unaffected by health warnings

was found to have converted his cell in another prison, with the consent of the governor, into a sort of luxury apartment with carpets and colour television. The bride was twenty-two-year-old Immacolata Jacone, sister of one of his henchmen also serving a long prison sentence for murder, whom he first met during a prison visit.

The wedding was widely reported in the Italian press. The bride wore white. She carried a spray of white gardenias, and there was champagne after the marriage ceremony at which both bride and groom received Holy Communion. Raffaele was not allowed to read his new wife a poem he had specially composed for the occasion in case it contained a message in code.

The boss of the Naples Camorra fancies himself as a poet and writer. His book *Poetry and Thoughts* circulates widely among inmates inside the Poggioreale prison in Naples, one of the main recruiting grounds for the New Camorra. An extract:

'A man who has no fear dies only once. The true member of the Camorra always reasons with his intelligence, never with his heart.

'My favourite flowers are orchids, but I often like to send chrysanthemums.

'We are the knights of the Camorra, men of honour, silence and sound principle.'

Raffaele Cutolo played a key role in the release of a political kidnap victim Ciro Cirillo, a local Christian Democrat Party worthy taken hostage in Naples by the Red Brigades terrorists in 1981. Emissaries from the Italian secret service visited Cutolo in his prison cell. Some time afterwards Cirillo was released, not far from the Poggioreale prison. The Red Brigades claimed that a ransom of over half-a-million pounds had been paid out of Christian Democrat Party funds. Cirillo himself said that not a penny of ransom was paid. Whatever was the exact truth about this shady affair, the uncrowned king of the Naples underworld was considered worth consulting by the highest organs of the Italian state in order to clear up a politically embarrassing crime.

In June 1983, the authorities did react. Ten thousand police rounded up 856 people in an unprecedented blitz against the Naples Camorra. Among them were wealthy businessmen and lawyers, the president of a soccer club, a pop singer, a nun, a prison chaplain, several mayors, and a well known national television personality. Raffaele's new wife Immacolata was also hauled inside.

A year later, 671 of the accused were sent for trial. The investigating magistrates found that 'at the beginning of the eighties the New Camorra had become a real national holding company funded by the profits of door-to-door extortion and the hijacking and robbery of container lorries'. The magistrates found that the Camorra was engaged in drug trafficking, the recycling of dirty money, and joint ventures with the Mafia and criminal organisations in other parts of Italy. It had placed its own men in local government, kept up regular contact with the political parties, and had infiltrated Naples society at all levels from big business and the professions, to the church, the world of entertainment, down to the teenage street gangs.

Among the accused was Sister Aldina Murelli, a fifty-one-year-old nun from the convent of the Daughters of Charity of the Most Precious Blood at Portici near Naples. Sister Aldina, known inside Raffaele's organisation as 'the Madonna', got to know 'the Professor' while trying to provide the comforts of religion to prisoners in Poggioreale. She may not have realised that she had entered a hornet's nest, and from the moment Raffaele presented her with a hefty cheque for her works of charity she became an energetic worker for the organisation. The nun carried letters in code in and out of prison hidden in the pages of her Bible. Police found letters reading 'The Madonna tells you . . . and the Saints must obey.'

Another of the accused was a jet-black-haired nightclub singer called Assunta Setaro, known to her friends as Alba. She acted as messenger for the Camorra's drug-trafficking division in the discos and nightclubs of Naples and was engaged to Raffaele's son Roberto. Yet another was Raffaele's chief legal adviser, a young man called Enrico Maddonna whom the boss had got to know in jail during one of his long prison spells, and whose legal studies he had paid for when Enrico was freed.

The Camorra relies heavily on ritual including blood-rites to perpetuate itself. Sixty per cent of those arrested bore a half-inch scar below the left-hand index finger indicating they had sworn blood-allegiance to the organisation. Much of the mumbo-jumbo uttered during these ceremonies was written by Don Raffaele himself. Police seized a recorded tape of what appeared to be an initiation ceremony during which Raffaele recalled the basic rules of the Camorra including the physical elimination of all its adversaries, and the masking of the identity of its members.

Police in Naples say that about half the fifty thousand shopkeepers in Naples have at one time or another paid protection money to the Camorra gangs. The technique for extortion is extremely simple. One or two Camorra men enter a shop pretending to sell matches, cigarette lighters or pens. They insist on a purchase. And the price usually turns out to be several hundred pounds, according to their victim's ability to pay.

One shopkeeper in the Via Roma, Naples' main shopping thoroughfare, who for obvious reasons preferred to remain anonymous, described an alternative approach.

'For thirty years,' he said, 'I have sold shoes and earned just enough to keep my wife, mother and three children.

'One morning a young man came in and asked to try on a pair of black shoes, size 43. Then he tried on various other kinds. He selected a pair and seemed satisfied. Then he said: "Thanks, but this is only on account" and walked out without paying.

'At that moment I realised I was on the Camorra's payroll list and would have to pay them regular "protection" money.'

Italians recognise that success in the prevention and punishment of crime in their country requires some radical reforms both of the police and the prison system. There has been agitation within the police for an end to the military law and discipline to which ordinary police officers were subject since the threat of a breakdown in public order during World War Two. This was accomplished in a law passed in 1981, which also provided for the creation of a Police Federation (police unions and the right to strike were forbidden under Italy's post-war constitution), and better co-ordination between the three different police forces, the public security force, the Carabinieri, and the Customs police. The prisons were the subject of two laws, in 1975 and 1977, which, on paper, created the basis for a new prison system which perhaps many wealthier and more socially advanced countries might envy.

The idea that prison was the place where society demanded retribution and punishment was to be substituted by a new concept that it should rehabilitate the criminal and prepare him for reinsertion into society. Each prisoner was to have his own cell, and there were ample provisions for alternatives to detention such as parole, half-time prisons, and a greater role for the social services.

These admirable plans have never been implemented; morale in some sections of the police remains low, while the prisons are literally bursting at the seams. The prison service is eight thousand men under strength; since the 'reform' there have been escapes, mutinies, suicides, and serious cases of violence inside the prisons, including several executions by prisoners themselves in a settling of accounts by rival gangs, not to mention the extraordinary goings on in the prisons where Raffaele Cutolo has been serving his current jail term.

Italy's prison population rose between 1979 and 1983 from twenty-eight thousand to over forty thousand which involved the cramming into the same cells of offenders of very differing degree, in conditions of degradation and promiscuity, particularly in many more antiquated prisons.

Such is the slowness of the judicial process, as mentioned in Chapter One, that two-thirds of prison inmates, at the latest count, were either awaiting trial, or final sentence.

This helps to explain the often equivocal attitudes of ordinary Italians from all parts of the peninsula, not only the neglected south, to crime and the law. On the one hand, Italians put crime as their number one preoccupation in a poll taken throughout the European Community. (In every other member state unemployment was the main worry.) On the other hand, a successful criminal or bandit who manages to defy the law arouses a certain admiration.

When the notorious boss of the Calabrian Mafia, Giuseppe Piromalli, sixty-three, was captured by police in February 1984 in Gioia Tauro after being on the run for nine years, there was a minor riot outside the police station where he was being held, by local people protesting at his arrest.

Piromalli was accused by the police of involvement in more than thirty murders during a prolonged war to the death between rival Mafia families.

But it was more important, in the eyes of his local friends and supporters, that for years he had been the Godfather of Gioia Tauro. He had enabled his business friends to take a rake-off from the huge sums of public money for engineering and public works contracts that had poured into this tiny Calabrian community as the result of a political decision in Rome.

Gioia had been chosen as the site for a major new steelworks, scrapped before it got off the drawing board when it became apparent that one thing Italy did not need during a world steel glut was more steel. The decision to abandon the project however was not taken until a huge port installation had been built by contractors controlled by the local Mafia.

An even more striking example of the local bandit being put on a pedestal was the case in 1979 of a Venetian bank robber killed in a dramatic duel with police in a motor boat chase through the canals of his native city.

Silvano Maistrello was a small-time petty criminal who grew up in a poor quarter of Venice and was in trouble with the police from the age of twelve. He graduated to bigger robberies, was arrested, but escaped no less than seven times from custody, leaping from a train, jumping out of the window of the police station where he was being interrogated, from courtrooms, and from jails. He became famous as the Houdini of Italian prisons.

But his luck ran out when he took part in a daylight raid on a bank near Saint Mark's Square. He got away, with only £15,000, in a small blue and white speedboat, but police in a faster boat pinned him down, and there was a gun battle with bullets whizzing in the air past startled tourists. Although Silvano was wearing a flak jacket a bullet pierced his heart and he died instantly. He was just thirty years old.

His funeral in the church near where he grew up was attended by a thousand mourners. Although the local press had expressed shock at the fact that Venice was 'becoming like Chicago, and will never more be an isolated backwater', Silvano was clearly regarded as a sort of local hero. His coffin was piled high with white roses, and little old ladies recounted tearfully to reporters how they remembered him, 'such a nice young boy' when he worked in the local milk shop.

As the funeral procession chugged slowly across the lagoon bearing Silvano to his final resting place in Venice's island cemetery, a small fleet of gondolas accompanied him.

FIVE

The Mayor of Montemilone

> Governing the Italians is not only impossible; it is useless.
>
> Benito Mussolini

When I first came to live in Italy at the beginning of the 1970s, I arrived in Rome armed with a sheaf of letters of introduction to members of the government and the establishment from an Italian friend in London, a correspondent whose name is a household word in Italy as he has reported from Britain for over fifteen years on RAI, the Italian State television and radio. It seemed like a tedious chore to go the rounds of a series of mainly political persons whose minds were clearly on matters far removed from the problems of a foreign correspondent settling down in a new country. But it quickly became apparent to me that it could be extremely useful, nay, necessary to equip myself in this country with what the natives call '*santi in paradiso*' – saints in heaven. Italian life is controlled by an interlocking series of old-boy networks of Byzantine complexity.

Politics in Italy is a power-game whose end product is normally not the public good, but the achievement of personal prestige, public status, a good job, and most important of all, enrichment by its practitioners, meaning potentially practically the whole adult male population. The long hand of the political parties stretches not merely into predictable fields like local government, but to banking, the media, public corporations, and even the appointment of the artistic director of leading opera houses.

The language of politics in Italy is confusing to foreigners because terms are used in a quite different sense to the synonyms in other languages and political systems. Parliamentary democracy does operate, it is true, but it would be foolish to compare proceedings in the Italian Senate with those in the House of Lords, or the Chamber of Deputies in Rome with the House of Commons in Westminster, or the role of Prime Minister with that of the Prime Minister of the United Kingdom or the President of the United States. An Italian Prime Minister, for example, holds office only as long as he remains *persona grata* to the leader of the party of 'relative majority' as it is called, the Christian Democrats, and is therefore less free to make important policy decisions than his counterparts in most other countries.

Ordinary Italians tend to find professional politicians exceedingly boring and the ten or twelve minutes of jargon which form the main item in the nightly RAI television newscast are endured by the watching millions more as a necessary penance than as offering any real enlightenment on the day's events. There is a deliberate cult of the enigmatic phrase among the nation's political élite. The late Aldo Moro, the former Christian Democrat Prime Minister and Party leader, invented a teaser called 'converging parallels' to explain the relationships within one of his coalition governments, while another Party leader, Ciriaco De Mita, managed to extract significant meaning out of what appeared to the uninitiated a quasi-theological discussion about the merits of 'the Establishment looking towards Society, or Society looking towards the Establishment'.

However politics does remain a matter of considerable importance to many Italians as very often it signals an open door towards that increasingly valuable commodity, a secure job in the public sector.

From the old age pensioner trying to establish his pension rights to the ambitious banker hoping to move into the top échelons of his profession, it can be extremely important which political party you belong to and who you know within that party. The three dominant parties in Italy are the Christian Democrats, the Communists and the Socialists, who carve up the important jobs between them, leaving the crumbs for the three other minor parties. The governing body of RAI, for example, is split up according to a formula actually fixed by law, which sounds like a telephone number – 643111. The Christian Democrats get six seats, the Communists four, the Socialists three and the minor parties one each.

There have only been two major changes of Italy's ruling classes within the past century. The first was in 1922 when the Fascists took over from the Liberals and the second in 1945 when the Anti-Fascists took over from the Fascists. In both cases the cause was external, the upheaval caused by a world war, so one can say that modern Italy has never known a genuine switch from one political class to another by ordinary democratic means. There have been innumerable redistributions of power among internal factions of the same ruling group, and the co-opting of minor groups by dominant ones, but all Italian governments are created on the basis that it is impossible, because of the system of proportional parliamentary representation and the proliferation of parties, to have proper alternative government switching between a true majority and a true opposition.

Political favouritism in Italy has been compared with the 'spoils system' in the United States whereby the winning party occupies certain posts in the administration. But the comparison is false because the appointees in the

United States know they will have to hand over their posts on the very day that their party has been voted out of office, while in Italy everyone who occupies a top job in the public or semi-public service knows that he could be there until retirement.

The whole of State capitalism in Italy, which means a very wide field indeed, covering nationalised oil and electricity, the big banks, and heavy industry including steel, cars, and chemicals, has been up for grabs by the political parties. Just because there are no swings and balances in Italian politics, the ideological old boy network of the parties overlays the whole system, throwing its organisational structure out of gear. And the nominee who owes his job to his party feels bound to recruit, favour and promote others designated by his party to the detriment of any productive organisation of goods and services.

A companion word to 'campanilismo' meaning attachment to one's native town, defined in Chapter One, is 'clientelismo' which means the master-servant relationship between the politician and those who support him in office. It is an ancient concept, which has survived any number of changes of political systems and governments, and its practice has been refined and honed to a point where it is extremely difficult for the average Italian to fix the point where 'clientelismo' ends and criminal corruption begins. Political scandals in Italy are a commonplace and of such staggering proportions that outsiders rub their eyes in astonishment on the rare occasions that the full details come out in court. Because the State is weak, it is considered fair game by ambitious operators like Licio Gelli, the Italo-Argentine Grand Master of a secret Freemasonry Lodge called P2, who managed to cream off some of the leading figures in Italy's military, judicial, diplomatic, police, intelligence, and parliamentary establishments, to create what has been correctly described as a state within the Italian state. Despite the formal outlawing of the P2 organisation, the setting-up of a parliamentary commission of enquiry into the scandal, the hasty transfer of a few officials, and the resignation of two government ministers, Gelli remains at large abroad, having even managed to bribe his way out of a Geneva prison after being arrested by the eagle-eyed Swiss.

Practically every major Italian city has some sort of criminal investigation going on into alleged corruption by its elected local administrators. Councillors belonging to all the major political parties have been clapped in handcuffs in an attempt by the judiciary to halt the spread of organised crime within local government. In 1983 alone, in Turin the deputy-mayor, a Socialist, his brother and three Socialist councillors were arrested on corruption charges; in San Remo the Christian Democrat mayor and five councillors ended up in jail in connection with charges relating to a two million pound sterling bribe (the judges said: 'Bribes are now a mass phenomenon, our enquiry simply reveals the system as it exists'); in Milan the world of high finance and publishing was under suspicion after the crash of the Banco Ambrosiano which had close links with the Vatican; in Florence the Socialist–Communist City council came under investigation for alleged maladministration; in Naples two Social Democrat councillors and one Republican Party worthy were convicted in connection with a racket involving the allocation of graves in the local cemetery, while a Communist went to gaol in connection with a bribery charge; and in Sicily a Republican party town councillor was arrested and gaoled in connection with the particularly unpleasant criminal case involving the kidnap for ransom of a seventeen-month-old baby girl, Elena Luisa, referred to in Chapter Four.

It would be unfair after this catalogue of crime to assume that dishonest administrators are the norm in Italy. Yet the picture I am painting of politics in action must take into account the somewhat murky atmosphere surrounding many aspects of the administration, both at local and national level.

In order to take a close look at how an Italian mayor operates, I travelled south to the province of Basilicata, in the heel of Italy, to meet Gerardo Labriola, Dino to his friends, mayor of Montelimone, a small agricultural town in one of the poorest and most thinly-populated parts of the peninsula. Basilicata, formerly known under its Roman name of Lucania, was a place of exile under Mussolini's dictatorship, and the painter and writer Carlo Levi who was sent there to rot during the 1930s produced a minor masterpiece of Italian twentieth-century literature *Cristo si è fermato a Eboli*, (*Christ stopped at Eboli*), about his experiences in a world of which many northern Italians still prefer to remain ignorant.

Over a century after the unification of Italy, many northern Italians still regard southerners as foreigners. Although official policy has been to pour cash into the economy of the poor south, to try to diminish the economic and cultural gap between the two halves of the country, that gap remains obstinately wide. When you arrive in the small '*comune*' of Montemilone the face of poverty is only too apparent. Montemilone is a jumble of village charm and concrete horror. It is also a town that is bleeding to death, being progressively abandoned by its inhabitants who can find no work and little satisfaction in a place which does not even boast a shoe shop, not to mention a cinema, or a disco.

Montemilone, perched a thousand feet above sea level on an escarpment overlooking the plains of Puglia, traces its history back to Roman times. It has been under occupation by various foreign armies, including those of Byzantium and Spain, but has just recently suffered a devastation that in human terms may have been greater than that caused by the wars and plagues of the Middle Ages, or by the earthquakes that periodically hit this part of Italy, the latest in 1980.

After remaining steady at between four-and-a-half and five thousand in the decade following the end of the Second World War, the population of Montemilone plummeted by half during the sixties and seventies as families fled not only to Italy's industrial north, but also to Switzerland, to West Germany, to Luxembourg, and even to America in search of work. Almost two thousand of the citizens of Montemilone (which now numbers, according to the 1981 census, only 2,660 souls), are aged sixty or over. In summer you see them sitting on the public benches waiting; in the words of Dino Labriola, 'like so many stranded turtles in the sun, waiting for death to arrive'. In winter the town seems dead. It only comes briefly to life when some of its frustrated youth appear in their cars or riding their motorbikes, roaring along the road to nowhere.

Dino, who looks like a younger and slighter version of Yves Montand, is in his early forties, and he's a mayor with a mission: to reverse the depopulation of his native town, to which he is deeply attached. He says he wants to improve the quality of life both for the old and the young but realises that he may just be tilting at windmills, given the background of inertia and neglect which pervades the whole south. Dino is a dedicated member of the Italian Communist Party, the second biggest political force in Italy which gets about thirty per cent of the total vote but is doomed to an apparently permanent role in opposition due to the peculiarities of the electoral system. Dino was elected mayor for the first time in 1979 after being asked to stand by his Party, and was re-elected in 1983 with seventy per cent of preference votes. If they are denied power at the national level, the Italian Communists argue, they must attack the problem at the grass roots – at local level. After electoral successes from 1976 onwards they took over the reins of local government in many principal cities in the north. But here in the south, Dino is odd man out – only about one mayor in ten is a Communist.

How does a highly motivated, competent administrator like Dino Labriola fare in a dying community like Montemilone, whose citizens, he says, are 'suffocated by fatalism'? Dino admits to bouts of pessimism. 'As a politician I feel impotent because I cannot give the right push to solve these problems within the time span allotted, and from a human point of view this is depressing. Life is very, very limited. This is a village which has been left to rot for a long time, in which not only the women but also the men gossip and have few social interests. This is disturbing because I have cultural aims, and it's a difficult running battle not to be brought down to their level.'

Dino was born in Montemilone, where his father was a local policeman, and in common with the majority of his contemporaries he migrated north to study and find work. He landed in Turin, became jack-of-all-trades, working for periods as a tailor and then in a bicycle factory. But he studied hard in his spare time, managed to obtain a university degree, and qualified as a teacher. Now he commutes each day by car during term time to teach in a secondary school in Melfi, a larger centre than Montemilone, about thirty miles away.

He has a long working day. Up at seven to drive to work in Melfi, back in the town hall by midday for two hours work in the mayor's office, lunch and a short siesta till four, then back to his administrative duties until about nine at night.

Dino is the product of two very different societies: urban, sophisticated Turin, where he spent twenty of his most satisfying years and the indolent south, and he sometimes gets quite excited about the possibilities of bringing the two opposite poles together. 'Just imagine if we were to irrigate a million hectares of land in southern Italy,' he fired at me, 'it would be as if a brand new FIAT car industry with 300,000 jobs came to be implanted here.'

Sitting in his office in the small, modern town hall just across the road from the flat where he lives with his wife Angela, also a Montemilone girl, and their two young children, he dealt rapidly with a succession of local problems brought along by his fellow citizens who clearly find Dino an accessible and effective administrator, and are not afraid to knock at his office door.

'I gained my experience of administration in the private sector and that's how I administer now as a public manager, by being punctual, by taking initiatives, by controlling spending, completing projects on time, by having the ability to give answers to those who are our customers, that is to say the people of Montemilone. I work up to ten hours a day and get very tired sometimes, and every day when I get home I am frustrated by the things I have not been able to accomplish, for the answers I could not give, and for the time I have taken away from my family.

'By being so much involved, by giving too much to others, I have had periods of grave family crisis. We are trying to get over this because I thought it was right to explain to my wife that what I do for others I am doing indirectly for my children too, to give them a better future and a better society to live in. It is just a drop in the ocean, and I suppose I cannot be taken as an example of the Italian way of doing things.'

Montemilone's 'First Lady' is clearly less than enchanted about her husband's commitment, and misses their previously more satisfying university life in the city of Turin.

'I was against coming back, knowing the mentality of the place here, and also knowing Dino. At first he came back by himself. Our marriage was quite seriously threatened. One year we only saw each other for a day or two at a time on three or four occasions. But we married because we loved each other sincerely, and the birth of the children reunited us.

'Being the "First Lady" of Montemilone, I have to keep up appearances, dress well, be nice to everybody. That's not my true character. I like sitting on the floor at home, or on the stairs. But this is my village where I was known long before all this happened, and I think deep down people quite like me because I don't give myself airs and graces.

'They used to call my elder boy "*Sindacchino*" [Little Mayor] and that used to annoy me, and then there was some bad feeling over picking him up for school from right outside the flat and not from the street corner like the other children – but this was because of his age not because he was a mayor's son.

'It is difficult to get away from Dino's job. He always brings papers home, and when we go out for a walk in the village people are always stopping us.

'Has Dino changed? He has become less open, perhaps it's the fault of politics. He's not so ready now to declare himself. My hopes for the children? Well, Montemilone doesn't offer us much, and since they are boys they need some prospects ahead of them, so my idea is to take them away from Montemilone eventually, to Rome or Turin, who knows?'

The coat of arms of Montemilone, displayed in Dino's office in embroidered glory on a large blue banner topped with brass knobs, carried in procession on ceremonial occasions, consists of a green oak tree standing on a hill with a wolf in the foreground. The heraldic device was invented during the period of the Spanish conquest of the Kingdom of Naples and this part of southern Italy in the sixteenth century. It recalls the dense forest land, populated by wolves, which once covered the area. Even as recently as the last century the people of Montemilone used to go hunting in the forest for wild boar, hares, porcupine, duck, woodcock and a wide variety of other game.

Now the trees have all gone, the landscape is bare, as the land has been ploughed up for cereal cultivation, the wolves are extinct, and at the present rate of emigration soon the land will be deserted by its inhabitants as well. But it will not be without a struggle on the part of Dino Labriola.

'Power can be maintained in two ways, through corruption or through participation,' Dino pontificated. 'We believe we have succeeded in showing that you can hold on to power by letting the people take part. It is an elevation of the political consciousness of the citizen.'

He went on to explain his political philosophy as a member of the Italian Communist Party. 'History shows there is no evolution without struggle by the people. I am referring, of course, not to the letting of blood, but to democratic struggles within the framework of a civil democratic relationship; but it is necessary to fight!

'What does Communism mean for me? It lies in the elevation of man to the role which history determines for him. Man can no longer be treated like a lemon to be thrown away once he has been squeezed. Some progress has been made towards this in the so-called Socialist countries, but the results are not entirely satisfactory. There must be a third way, which takes the positive aspects of both Socialism and Capitalism and builds a new society where man is the main object and beneficiary of society.'

Dino's brave new world of Marxist jargon is not viewed with a sympathetic eye by Montemilone's parish priest, Father Francesco Aliberti, who lives next door to the church in the former Piazza of the Sacred Heart at the opposite end of town to the Labriolas. One of the first acts of the new Communist-led town council upon its election in 1979 was to secularise the Piazza, to rename it in memory of the emigrants, absent heroes whose loss is felt so deeply by those who remain behind. Dino commissioned a gigantic mural painting fifteen feet high and fifty feet long to embellish the new 'Piazza degli Emigrati'. It depicts a group of peasants bowed by toil in the fields, a bad local Baron, the former big landowner, and a family packing up their chattels ready to leave Montemilone. The mural, an unashamed piece of political art, faces the church, and would confront Father Francesco's congregations every time they went to Mass, if his church had not been seriously damaged in the earthquake of 1980, since when it has been closed.

His dimishing flock now gathers in another nearby church where the cracks caused by the earthquake are still apparent, but there is no imminent danger of the building collapsing. I saw mostly children and over-sixties in the congregation of about a hundred. What particularly caught my eye however was a small brass plate on one of the pews. It bore the name Labriola.

After his Mass I talked to Father Francesco in his poverty-stricken house next door to the old church now in disuse. I asked him about relations with the mayor, who used to be a regular attender at Mass when he was a boy. 'Politics is a whore!' he exclaimed. 'The young people all go away because the only jobs available here are in the gift of the mayor and his Party. If you have a Party card you can get a job even if you are a cretin. I get angry because it's the young men who are least qualified who get the handful of jobs handed out by the 'comune'. The rest have to leave to find work. Last year seventeen young men volunteered either for the army or the carabinieri police. It's a handicap for us priests to see the departure of all this youthful energy.'

But then he softened a little. 'I used to be a friend of Dino Labriola, and I am sorry there is no longer this collaboration now he is mayor.' And he admitted rather grudgingly: 'Perhaps power has changed him. But he really does care about the town and he's getting things done. We have to recognise a certain commitment on the part of the present town council.'

Father Francesco appeared resigned to the inevitability of the slow decline of Montemilone, despite what he believes are the high religious principles of its population. He told me with some pride that there are no civil weddings in Montemilone, everyone still gets married in church, but lamented the fact that of seventeen couples he married in 1982, ten left town for good to begin new lives elsewhere in Italy, while in 1983 eight out of fourteen couples left. The parish register records the vital statistics of decline. Deaths now outnumber births by two to one.

Father Francesco complained that Dino the mayor had managed to get full compensation from government funds for all the homes and public buildings damaged in the 1980 earthquake, while his own main church remains boarded up and abandoned to the elements. During the 1983 local election campaign, the priest was so incensed by Dino's speech at one public meeting that he denounced the mayor for blasphemy to the police. (What Dino actually said, using a play on words, was 'Dio perdona, ma Dino non perdona mai!', (God forgives, but Dino never forgives!)

The reason for the prompt receipt of compensation by Montemilone, which was not near the epicentre of the earthquake, while much more badly damaged *comuni* were still waiting for funds, lay in Dino's skill as an administrator. He got his town declared a disaster area, 'not for dishonest campanilistic reasons, but in order to defend the legitimate rights of the citizens', in the words of a progress report put out by the town hall.

Dino's brushes with higher authority and central government reflect the tenacious and all-pervading role of the Christian Democrat Party hierarchy over most of southern Italy.

'The bureaucracy in Italy acts as a brake, not as a motor system to serve the community. You are tied to the State not as an abstract entity, but to State power, which is something quite different and has been in the gift of the Christian Democrats here for thirty-five years. This party puts the brake on everything.

'I think that democracy could be revitalised by the alternation of power between different political forces. We won the election here because our programme was better than that of our predecessors.'

Dino Labriola's main battleground with State power during his term as mayor has been the site for a new forty-million-pound dam a mile down the road from Montemilone.

The dam is being built astride land owned partly by Montemilone and partly by a neighbouring *comune*. Dino organised sit-in demonstrations with banners to ensure that some of the benefits of this vast engineering project on his very doorstep should be enjoyed by his fellow citizens. In an area chronically short of water for irrigation of land and even for drinking, it seemed unjust to him that Montemilone was never even consulted when the plans were drawn up.

'It just shows how contemptuous central government is of local authorities, and bypasses them even when it's a question of an extremely important project like the dam,' Dino explained.

'The two towns concerned were never consulted at the planning stage. We wanted to find out how much water we could get for irrigation, what sort of safety precautions would be adopted. We made a fuss because it seemed absurd to us that we should not be consulted. We did finally get satisfactory answers about safety, but not about the employment of local labour.

'It's all part of a deliberate policy, it is not a matter of ignorance. In Italy, you see, the authorities often claim that they never knew the facts. General Dalla Chiesa, the man who defeated the Red Brigades terrorists and who was sent to fight the Mafia, gets killed and they say they didn't know the facts leading up to his murder; Michele Sindona, serving a twenty-five year sentence in the United States for bank fraud, organises a fake kidnap and they don't know the circumstances; Licio Gelli, the master mind of the P2 Freemasons Lodge, escapes from gaol in Geneva and they don't know the facts. The Milan Bank bomb in Piazza Fontana: fifteen years later they still have not found out who carried out the massacre. Roberto Calvi, the banker, is found hanged under a bridge in London and no one knows anything.

'Now if someone comes up to me and says: Mr Mayor, in Montemilone such and such has happened, and I say I don't know anything about it, he would ask me to my face what on earth I am supposed to be doing then as Mayor. I cannot fail to answer for the actions of my subordinates. I am the one who is responsible. If I am not able to reply it means I have not been doing my job properly.

'How can a minister or a government fail to give precise answers? How can they permit a project like the dam to go ahead without giving a new chance to these underdeveloped areas which have been left to rot for years?

'The reason is that it is convenient for those in power to deal in aid and influence, to practice "clientelismo".

'If we have before us people without the security of a job, they will always be bound to doff their caps and kowtow to us. If on the other hand we free these people from the unequal power relationship between those who govern and those who are governed, they will greet us civilly, but not feel under our thumb. These are the factors which ought to influence development in southern Italy but which unfortunately do not.'

The sense of frustration experienced by Dino came through strongly as we walked on a winter's day through the windswept main street of Montemilone. He expounded: 'There's a cultural problem to solve here, not only a structural problem; how do you react to a world that's passive and inert?

'I am sad and pessimistic by nature, even though my ways might seem like those of an optimist. I am terribly pessimistic – all you have to do is to look at the history of this place.'

Indeed as you approach Montemilone across a desolate landscape almost devoid of trees, it looks as if a war has passed over the countryside. A group of gutted houses, a rubbish dump and the cemetery are the first landmarks.

The cemetery is being extended, not only because of the high mortality rate, and the ageing population, but because scores of migrants from Montemilone now living in Luxembourg, West Germany, Belgium, Turin or Milan want the assurance that at least they can return home when they are dead, and have booked space for their tombs.

Visiting the graves of one's family is an ancient ritual that is still very important to the older inhabitants of Montemilone. When Dino became mayor, he noticed how the old people had to walk the two miles from town to the cemetery to put their flowers on the graves. So he authorised the school bus, once it had taken the children to school in the morning, to pick up old people who were unable to walk so far and to bring them back again home.

Dino told me: 'I often come to the cemetery when I have a problem to solve. I find dead friends and relations, and the tombs are silent, they cannot answer me, just as the people buried there could not answer me during the years when they were away from Montemilone in their own lifetime.

'It is a moment for profound reflection; death is inevitable, but it is obvious that one can live a better life by giving oneself to others while one is still alive.

'The tomb represents continuity. We have a long tradition in Italy of the presence of the individual tomb, celebrated in particular by an eighteenth-century Milanese poet called Giuseppe Parini who condemned the French for digging mass graves for the dead when they overran Italy. Parini praises the individual tomb because it represents the continuation of man's presence even after his death. And relations visiting the tomb can continue to communicate even if the dead person cannot reply.'

Dino goes each year to visit his living compatriots abroad and each year, too, many of them return to the homes they left behind for just a few weeks in summer to keep contact with their roots. The migrants usually also return home to vote at election time as there is no system of proxy voting in Italy, and the government provides free transport to the voter's home town from the frontier when once they have arrived back on Italian territory. Dino showed me a letter he received from a citizen of Montemilone who has kept a barber's shop in the Bronx in New York for over three decades. Seventy-two-year-old Nicola d'Amelio wrote to say he was coming back home for a month or two to cure his debilitating asthma and to get away from what he called 'this dreadful American climate'.

Dino said he would like to visit his fellow citizens in the United States, clearly not without a certain self-interest for the votes this might bring him, but when I met him he had a problem in getting his passport from the authorities. During his term as mayor he has appeared in court no less than thirty-five times to answer charges brought by various disgruntled political opponents, including Father Francesco; under Italian law as long as any of these cases were pending, his passport could be withheld.

But Dino's problems as chief executive of Montemilone are child's play in comparison with those of the mayor of southern Italy's largest city, Naples.

Maurizio Valenzi, seventy-four, is visibly worn out by his eight-year term as head of a city council which started out full of enthusiasm but was defeated by the dead weight of centuries of misrule by Spanish viceroys, Bourbon kings, and latterly, corrupt Neapolitan family clans, not to mention the Camorra.

The Communists in Naples began, with excellent intentions, a clean-up campaign involving the purchase of several hundred of the latest in mechanised dustcarts and roadsweepers, and the dynamiting of blocks of apartments erected without proper building licences.

80 *Italians*

Neither of these imaginative steps came to anything. The dustcarts were systematically sabotaged by sanitation department employees who filled the motors with sand, or vandalised the hi-tech equipment in order to get more pay or work less hours, leaving the rubbish to accumulate high in the streets, with all the attendant risks of creating a major epidemic. Cholera is still not unknown in Naples.

The concrete jungle which disfigures the former natural beauty of the Bay of Naples continues its relentless spread. Building speculators were undeterred by a stick or two of official dynamite as long as there were high profits to be earned. Three-quarters of the shops in Naples are reported to be paying protection money to local racketeers, despite some massive protest demonstrations by shopkeepers which led to the city virtually closing down for several days in 1983.

'We realised,' Mayor Valenzi said, 'that it was impossible to administer Naples legally. For example, in order to make town hall employees work a full day (which in Italy only means half-a-day as practically everybody in local and national government offices clocks off at the latest by two in the afternoon), we had to pay them overtime. The Special Government Commissioner (sent to run Naples when the Communists resigned) made an official complaint but then had to pay up as well, otherwise there wouldn't even have been an usher to open the door when he arrived at his office.'

The square in front of the Naples Town Hall for years has been the scene of practically daily demonstrations by the unemployed, the homeless, the flotsam and jetsam of a society that often seems to be on the brink of total anarchy, but which connoisseurs of the Italian scene know has infinite capacities of survival.

One day, Mayor Valenzi was faced by a phalanx of two hundred yellow city cabs drawn up in front of his town hall in protest against the number of unlicensed taxis operating. He received a drivers' delegation and signed a decree to protect their livelihood.

Two days later the mayor's secretary knocked at his door with a distraught face. 'Mr Mayor, there are four hundred yellow cab drivers demonstrating in front of the town hall.'

'I thought we had dealt with them already.'

'Yes, but these are the unlicensed cab drivers!'

A banner was strung above the sea of hooting taxis. It read: 'UNLICENSED, YES! STARVING TO DEATH, NO!'

The mayor did a deal, Neapolitan-style.

If Naples suffers from problems of disorderly growth, Genoa, Italy's largest port city, over four hundred miles to the north, suffers from hardening of the arteries.

It is the only major Italian city which has remained, demographically speaking, stagnant since the Second World War. It was the city which built the last of the great Italian transatlantic liners, the *Leonardo da Vinci* and the *Rafaello*, which became obsolete through the rise in air travel while they were still on the drawing board, and had to be sold off as floating hotels. Genoa is a monument to the failure of Italian State capitalism with its huge and ailing steel industry. Even the port is only a shadow of what it could be, having failed to adapt itself to the needs of modern container traffic.

Part of the reason is geography; Genoa is cut off by mountains, despite the building of motorways linking the city by tunnel with the rest of the country. But the local power structure may also bear some responsibility for the ossification of the former great maritime Republic.

The real power in Genoa lies not in the hands of the democratically-elected city council but in the person of the ageing Cardinal Archbishop Giuseppe Siri. Cardinal Siri has reigned over Genoa since the end of the Second World War. He has twice come near to election as Pope, and has twice been frustrated in his ambitions. He was created Cardinal by Pope Pius XII in 1953 and saw himself as transition Pope when Pius died in 1958. But the mood of the rest of the Roman Catholic Church was against him. Pope John XXIII was elected instead and Cardinal Siri has now come to be identified in ecclesiastical terms with the forces of opposition to the reforms of the Second Vatican Council.

In secular affairs the Cardinal has come to be seen in Genoa as a politically powerful figure comparable to the Prince-Bishops of the eighteenth century in central Europe. Many of the captains of Italy's State industries owe their careers to him. When the Communists and Socialists won the local election in 1975 and came to power for the first time in Genoa, they reached a compromise with the Cardinal who remains a constant point of reference in all matters concerning the city.

But the Cardinal has an outspoken critic, a local Roman Catholic priest called Father Gianni Baget Bozzo, who has drawn public attention to what he considers a lamentable state of affairs in Genoa in frequent editorials in the national press.

'In Genoa,' wrote the priest, 'Cardinal Siri is not a bishop like other bishops. He does not represent the people, he expresses a power. The IRI [Italy's powerful State industrial holdings company] has been negotiating with him for decades.

'Power in Genoa has escaped from all forms of public control and is split up into secret agreements between different interest groups which are each concerned only with their own little world, with no one caring about the whole.

'It is significant that the Church and Freemasonry have found it easy to reach compromises despite their historic conflicts of principle. Perhaps the explanation can be found in the unremovable Cardinal who confers legitimacy upon what the Spanish used to call '*poderes facticos*' or real powers in Genoa.'

It is only fair to add that Father Baget Bozzo has become something of a political priest himself. He was elected to the European Parliament as a Socialist in the 1984 European elections. The Italian Socialist Party congress had given him a standing ovation when he announced he was standing as their candidate. The Vatican, following the rigid instructions of Pope John Paul II, who reserves to himself the sole right to practise Church politics, began disciplinary proceedings against Father Baget Bozzo, who is likely to be suspended from his priestly functions.

But he is unrepentant. 'I have gone into politics,' he told me, 'because I am convinced that the Church itself must not be a political power. What is needed is the personal commitment of all Christians individually. Religion has been pushed to one side by our society and there is a radical separation between the clergy and real life. Christianity itself must become a political community otherwise it is finished.'

One man who holds undisputed power in Italy is Romano Prodi the current head of IRI, the State holding company which was set up under the Mussolini regime to rescue the Italian banking system after the great international Wall Street crash. Today, IRI employs over half-a-million Italians, carries out a third of the entire research and development in Italian industry and owns six per cent of Italy's total assets. It has major interests in banking, steel, ship-building, food, telecommunications, and owns the state airline *Alitalia* and the state television and radio corporation RAI.

Romano Prodi who is in his mid-forties, young for a top Italian, was launched on a successful academic career by a scholarship at the London School of Economics.

I asked him what in his view was the quality which enabled Italians to exercise power successfully. 'Compromise,' he replied, 'we have a great capacity for compromise. The style of negotiating here is very different from that in France or Britain.

'Take the European steel crisis for example. The implications for Italy of the decline of the steel industry are just as bad as for Britain or France, but the worst industrial unrest in steel broke out in France, not here. Why? Because when I go to Genoa to sort things out, everyone, the management and the unions realise that there is a price to pay and we reach an agreement.

'But we pay a high price for the divisions and fragmentation of our country. Every small step forward collectively is the result of a full-scale war.

'Tactics and cunning are what seize the imagination of Italians. We are not so much interested in where the point of arrival is, as in how you reach it. The conduct of business is frequently all tactics and no final goal.

'From my point of view Italy's most worrying feature is the low level of the operational capacity of the State and of government in particular.

'It may be true to say that it is precisely because the State is so weak that Italian society is so much alive and has such an ability to innovate. But I am personally convinced that without the capacity to propose and implement large-scale projects Italian society does not have a very promising future ahead of it, neither will it write much history.

'Spontaneous vitality may lead to a greater capacity to adapt, as indeed has happened in the past. Italy is an excellent example of "social do-it-yourself". But without large-scale projects, without collective goals, without an enhancement of the system, Italy will increasingly remain an object of curiosity to historians and social scientists, and less an effective protagonist in its economic and political affairs, and will therefore lose its hold on its own future.'

A sober assessment from one who knows the realities of State power in Italy from the inside.

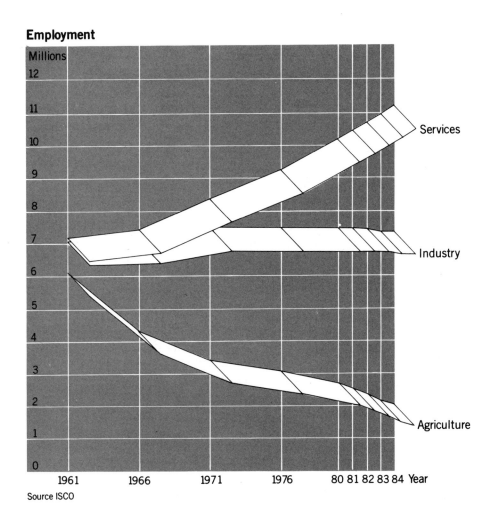

Employment

Source ISCO

SIX

The Fatal Gift of Beauty

> Italia, oh Italia thou who hast
> The fatal gift of beauty.
>
> Byron
> *Childe Harold's Pilgrimage*
>
> *Deh fossi tu men bella e almen più forte!*
> God, if only you were less beautiful and just a little stronger.
>
> Vincenzo Filicaia, Florentine poet 1642–1707

I always marvel when I land in Rome after flying in from murkier climes, at the luminosity of everything. It is as if hitherto I had been living in the semi-darkness and suddenly someone had switched on the light.

Italy is an intensely visual country. People and things are judged first and foremost on their appearances. *'Fare bella figura'*, literally to make a fine show or not to lose face, is a requirement as much of good behaviour as of aesthetics. And the opposite, *'fare brutta figura'*, is something to be avoided at all costs in the minds of all Italians. I feel sure that it is the special qualities of the light that have caused the visual arts to flower in Italy as in no other country in Europe. Strong sunlight creates colour, casts shadows, raises perspective. Although it is the delicately-coloured fresco paintings of the late Middle Ages, and the more boldly-coloured art of the Renaissance that has traditionally attracted visitors from beyond the Alps to the churches and picture galleries of Italy, a whole brilliantly-coloured world of painting that once embellished the public and private buildings of ancient Rome has been almost entirely lost to us. It is difficult today to imagine Trajan's huge sculpted marble column in Rome, which illustrates the Emperor's military campaigns and victories, as a sort of illuminated manuscript of the first century AD glowing with reds, blues and yellows. Now it is grey with atmospheric pollution, and mostly hidden by scaffolding from public gaze as technicians prepare to sand-blast away whatever vestiges of colour might have survived.

Ancient Greece and Rome were polychrome civilisations. The statues of Praxiteles were referred to by the Greeks, and by the Romans who copied them, by their colours. They talked about the 'violet of the eyes' of one famous piece of antique sculpture. Our perception of the ancient world is coloured, or perhaps one should more correctly say blanched, by the purist concepts of foreigners like Winckelmann, who saw the buildings and portrait busts of ancient Rome in falsely pure tones of black and white. Not that the Romans themselves were insensitive to the qualities of reflected light. Latin has two separate words to describe different shades of both black and white: *niger* means shiny black while *ater* refers to a matt kind of dull black; *albus* conveys the idea of a dull egg-white, while *candidus* means brilliant white like snow.

Modern Italians have a sensitivity to colour and to design that is reflected in the way they dress. The fashion industry earns more than £4,000 million just in domestic sales each year, and design is considered important not just by industrialists anxious to increase their sales, but by teenagers avid to follow their own fashions. Even punk styles imported from Britain undergo a subtle change when adopted by Italian youth. The haircuts, the make-up are all more carefully thought out and applied than in the original product. The desire to shock is modified because it has also to meet the requirements of *bella figura*.

Italy is strewn with remains from the past abandoned by generations convinced they could do, or knew, better. There are still two million houses standing dating from between 1300 and 1700 and most of them are in poor repair. Ancient buildings, pieces of sculpture and paintings are so abundant that Italians have become completely blasé about their artistic heritage. The foreigners set up charitable funds to Save Venice and labour with love to restore crumbling buildings, while the locals invent grandiose schemes, pass laws, and then proceed to forget all about propping up the past. Great Italian artists have never hesitated to tear down or paint on top of the works of their predecessors. Raphael for example painted frescoes on top of works by Piero della Francesca when he was decorating the Vatican. Old Saint Peter's with its monuments and memories of over a thousand years of mediaeval history was unceremonially torn down and replaced with the present Basilica by a series of sixteenth-century Popes who may have been patrons of Michelangelo but would have been regarded as vandals by modern conservationists.

The marbles of Greek temples have been transformed into lime by peasants, Roman amphitheatres have been turned into fortresses by ambitious princes, or used as stone quarries, invading armies from the north led by Huns, Goths, Napoleon and the Nazis have pillaged, destroyed and looted to their fill, American millionaires and foreign museum curators have in our time taken their pick of what survived the various holocausts of the past. And still the storerooms of Italy's museums are stuffed with hidden treasure.

Only one-third of the paintings, pieces of sculpture and *objets d'art* owned by the Italian State are on permanent public display. Two-thirds are kept permanently locked away or put on only periodic show. One-third of the nation's museums are closed for lack of custodians. The rest tend to open only in the mornings and large sections are frequently closed either for restoration or because there are not enough museum staff to guarantee security.

The Italian State pays a miserable few million pounds each year for the upkeep of what could be one of the nation's biggest tourist attractions. It has been suggested that the galleries and museums ought to be handed over to private enterprise, but I know only too well this is no solution either. I happen to live in one of Rome's former private museums, which used to house the collection of antique marbles of Prince Torlonia, a nineteenth-century nobleman belonging to the family whose fortunes were made by supplying victuals to Napoleon's invading armies. The present prince decided to convert the museum into private apartments for rent, and locked away the sculpture, more than six hundred pieces both Greek and Roman. For forty years this unique collection has been unavailable either to scholars or to the general public. The Rome City Council has declared its intention of issuing a compulsory purchase order for the collection and installing it in a worthy setting, but for the foreseeable future the money for such a laudable purpose is simply not available. When it actually comes to finding cash for preserving the cultural heritage upon which so many fine words are lavished, the politicians who control Italy's purse-strings realise that neither Praxiteles nor Raphael nor Michelangelo have any votes to offer, and therefore the Culture Ministry remains the Cinderella of all government departments.

Fortunately, however, official Italy represents only one side of the coin.

I travelled to Prato, near Florence, to meet an Italian who has devoted his life (he is now a spry seventy-six) to the care and protection and to the resuscitation of some of the most important and rare and exquisite paintings in the whole field of Western art. I am referring here to the fresco paintings of the thirteenth, fourteenth and fifteenth centuries on the walls of churches, monasteries and public buildings, in Tuscany mainly, but also in other parts of Italy.

The fresco artist used to mix his colours and then apply them direct on to the wall on top of a fine white plaster base while the plaster was still wet. The technique demanded extremely rapid work as once the wall was dry additions or alterations could only be made using tempera colours which give a different result. If you look carefully at a mural by a master such as Giotto you can tell exactly how many days he took to complete the painting. Each 'day' covers a clearly delineated area which had to be completed before the plaster dried.

The techniques of mediaeval fresco painting (which incidentally were quite different from those used by the mural decorators of ancient Pompeii) have only been studied systematically with the benefit of chemical analysis during the past two decades. Much remains to be understood, but Leonetto Tintori is one of a very small élite of Italian restorers who has a comprehensive grasp of what is really a lost art. He gained his immense knowledge and skill through spending long years crouched over the works of such masters as Giotto, Filippo Lippi and Duccio, whose survival has been particularly threatened this century by war damage, neglect, damp and now, most serious of all, atmospheric pollution.

Leonetto Tintori now lives in semi-retirement in a villa among the olive groves which cover the hillsides around Prato, the prosperous small Tuscan town whose fortunes were founded on the cloth and wool trade seven hundred years ago. What immediately struck me as he showed me photographs of some of his major restorations, was that for him our modern distinction between artist and craftsman made as little sense as it would to Giotto himself.

'I worry a lot about the state of mural paintings in Italy which is really terrible,' he told me. 'Damage has been piled upon damage. In the eighteenth century there was often excessive cleaning and over-painting. Then, later, two schools of thought developed – one led by the antique dealers who wanted to produce a nice bright object that would sell, and another, much encouraged by the Germans, who believed in liberating a painting completely from the accretions of time and of man.

'Both views are wrong. A good restoration is only rarely achieved. The restorer must not intrude, nor work mechanically.

'The most important phase in conservation is the cleaning. It is easy to remove varnishes, but difficult to save the patina, that egg-white finish applied by the artist which often became slightly greyish on drying, but which unified the whole composition.

'The patina is not something acquired in time, but the painter's own finish. The fundamental idea in restoration is as far as possible to restore the authenticity of the work, to reinforce the colours, and bring together what is left of the original.'

Leonetto explained to me that where there were gaps through damage, he always tried to work on them in a way which respected the original.

'You must never fake it. The additions must always be distinguishable. Sometimes it may be a good idea to leave a totally blank space, without even indicating what might have been there, so as not to distract from what little is left. In other cases it may be best to complete the main lines of the composition and allow the use of a little colour. In general it is as well for repainting not to predominate, even when you can distinguish it, because it is a sort of pollution which never has the luminosity or the meaning of the original. It is something quite different however well done it is.'

Leonetto left school when he was only twelve years old, and after sundry jobs, including working in a textile factory and as a haberdasher's assistant (which he hated), began learning about mural paintings in the most modest of ways – as a distemperer of walls, a house painter. He did his apprenticeship as a restorer the hard way, on a scaffolding in the transept of the cathedral in his own home town where he spent three years helping to bring back to life the Gothic ceiling, in a project financed by the local Savings Bank. He was then twenty-five and reflected somewhat ruefully that at that age Giotto was already covering the Church of Saint Francis in Assisi with his sublime frescoes.

'Working in Prato cathedral I learned about the sense of commitment which is essential for a restorer, without which he remains just a technician; commitment is the key to our work. And modesty, so that you don't impose your own personality upon the work you are restoring. And respect for your colleagues and recognition of their qualities even if sometimes you don't agree with their point of view.

'I could have earned a lot more money than I allowed myself to, but I didn't want to compromise on quality. Of course when you commit yourself deeply to restoration it cannot be a source of wealth, only if you work in a superficial way with results, as you can imagine, that don't last long.

'A good restorer must really know the materials he is working with. It probably doesn't matter if he is not interested in history or art criticism, but he does have to have a real grasp of the practicalities of the art. A lot of restorers go wrong because they devote themselves to selling the product or to the scientific side which is not their real job.'

I travelled with Leonetto to a small country chapel in the rolling countryside near Siena at a hamlet called Montemaggio. Some mural paintings had been discovered there dating from the thirteenth century. They were hidden under a coat of whitewash, and Leonetto believed they might be by the great master Duccio himself.

'In these little country churches,' he said, 'you can often make spectacular finds. They may only be small but they are of the highest quality. They have been built to merge in with the countryside and with the neighbouring houses, still inhabited by peasants today.

'Buildings were often covered, inside and out, with whitewash when people were trying to protect themselves against the plague. And when people fancied having a new picture, they didn't stop to think about repainting the old one, they just slapped a new one on top. There are one or two fifteenth-century paintings on top of thirteenth-century ones here. We can't be sure of saving them because they have been hammered. Some restoration has already been done, and irreparable mistakes were made in uncovering the frescoes. A knife was used which scratched the original paint. Then in order to cover up their destruction, they put new paint on top which distorted the original, not only its contours, but its whole appearance. In this simple architecture, light and very soft colours from the end of the thirteenth century look best, not the harsh colours used in the twentieth century.

'The architecture of the shrines and chapels of the countryside tells of sincere faith, of the simple life, full of light and sun and good health. I always prefer simple things. To live here with farm workers would be a real pleasure for me. I'd go and drink their wine and their *vin santo*, they make wonderful *vin santo*.

'The landowners who are left here are no longer authoritarian princes but ordinary people who often work side by side with the peasants, and even spend their own money to protect these works of art. These paintings might well have been destroyed if they had belonged to a prince, but in fact the peasants and the small landowner have done all they could to prevent rain from getting in, and made sure there was glass in the windows. So they managed to preserve it right down until our day and now it is a real duty on our part not to jeopardise all the care they have taken.'

I asked Leonetto how much it would cost to restore the paintings in this small chapel. About seventy thousand pounds sterling at current exchange rates he told me.

'We would need five or six people for eight months and they would have to move here from the town and sleep away from home. You can't take local craftsmen. No private person around here could raise the amount needed. And the State has many things to spend money on, even though this would only cost the equivalent of six feet of motorway. The State thinks motorways are important and cannot find enough cash for art in the countryside.'

Arrangements for financing the restoration of the whole chapel fell through; a private foundation in Venice finally provided one-twentieth of the original estimate, enough just to bring back to life one haloed thirteenth-century Madonna.

Leonetto agonises over past failures to salvage the saveable, but is proud of what he has done, sometimes in the face of official disapproval, to rescue frescoes from destruction.

His greatest triumph was the piecing together of a fresco painting of the Madonna and Saints by Filippino Lippi done in 1497 at a shrine next to the artist's house in Prato which received a direct hit from an Allied bomb in 1943.

The authorities had built a protective wall of bricks, but this was insufficient to save the painting which was lying in pieces on the ground when Leonetto arrived.

'I heard about the bombing from a peasant, jumped on my bicycle and raced to Filippino's house. There was incredible confusion. I turned to the city authorities for help but they actually threatened me with deportation if I did anything. So I found a tarpaulin from a nearby slaughterhouse to protect the fragments from damp and further damage. Luckily the whole fresco was scattered within an area of only five or six metres. I stuck a gauze backing on to the larger pieces and packed the smaller pieces away in sand, just like sardines in a box. Within twenty days all the pieces had been recovered. I took them to an empty villa near my home and day by day, month by month, I gradually fitted them together again.

'Many other frescoes were destroyed by bombing about this time, in Padua, in Viterbo, at the monumental cemetery in Pisa, but in no other case were precautions taken like those I took in Prato, so that when the time came round to try to reconstruct them it was too late.'

The incendiary bomb which devastated the monumental cemetery just near the leaning tower in Pisa put at risk a famous series of huge mural paintings depicting whole cycles of bible history.

Leonetto found a tragic scene when he arrived.

'It was November, cold and damp, a desolate atmosphere. Military tarpaulins had been placed over the damaged frescoes as some protection against the insistent rain. We carried out some first aid, but the plaster, swollen with humidity, was flaking off in great lumps. The only way of saving the frescoes was to detach them by glueing a cloth fronting on to them and stripping the whole painting away from the wall. Then they were stuck to a new stable backing, usually hardboard, but techniques were not as developed as they are nowadays.'

One of the most striking frescoes in Pisa is called the Triumph of Death. It shows a fourteenth-century Tuscan nobleman and his ladies out on a hunting expedition. Suddenly they come upon an apocalyptic scene. Bodies rise from their tombs. Devils drag finely bedecked members of the court down to the Inferno. Thanks to Leonetto's efforts you can still see it today. He described to me how it was saved.

'The backing which separated the Triumph of Death from the wall had been semi-carbonised and something had to be done quickly as the plaster was all flaking off. The weather was relentless. After three or four days you could see patches of mould developing. I couldn't sleep at night until I urged the superintendent of antiquities to provide a means of drying it artificially. We borrowed some awnings and tried to apply heat from underneath. And then suddenly the weather changed. The cold dry wind from the mountains, the Tramontana, started to blow and in a single day we took down the Triumph of Death.'

Most of the frescoes from Pisa which survived the fire have succumbed to atmospheric damage in the years since the Second World War.

'If the inexcusable stubbornness of the people in control had not condemned the frescoes stripped from the wall to be put on show without adequate protection, we could still have the masterpieces of Benozzo Gozzoli and Piero di Puccio in a viewable state in some gallery today,' Leonetto complained. 'You only have to compare the Triumph of Death, which was protected, with the horrible state of most of the frescoes of the Pisa cemetery today to realise who is responsible.'

Leonetto went abroad for help, to researchers in New York and Pittsburgh, when he received what he considered inadequate scientific back-up from the Italian State authorities. The Italians, he said, suffered from 'paralysing personal susceptibilities and conflicts'.

'It was not until the 1960s that the major cause of the deterioration of fresco paintings – sulphurisation – was recognised. But twenty years have gone by and nothing has been done either in the light of my recommendations or in the light of subsequent discoveries. It is useless to carry out complex cleaning operations and put frescoes back without adequate protection, which means temperature and humidity controls. Frescoes which have been stripped off for restoration must not be allowed to moulder away during decades in museum storerooms.'

The disastrous flood in Florence in 1966 which destroyed thousands of irreplaceable paintings, manuscripts, and frescoes found Leonetto Tintori back in an emergency situation, lending his expertise. But it was not always appreciated by the powers that be.

'When I arrived in Florence it was utter chaos. All the works were dirtied with oil, soaked in water, overturned and even smashed. It was a really tragic situation if you think how fragile a work of art is. It was really more than I could bear, enough to make you cry.

'Canvases and wood panels were first of all protected with acrylic resin and then taken for drying out to the *Limonaia*, a sort of decompression chamber where they were supposed to be dried slowly in a controlled temperature. But independent operators like me were kept out. I experimented with sand, which successfully prevented the crystallisation of salts while frescoes were drying, and with blotting paper on wood panels. I spoke very often about my experiments to the authorities in Florence, but by the time I was convinced of the success of my system, it was too late to change the whole system they had worked out. So my advice went to waste.

'Together with the most spontaneous demonstrations of goodwill and spirit of sacrifice, the meanest weaknesses of human nature came out at such an inopportune moment. Questions of who was in charge, presumptuous behaviour, resentment and ambition polluted the atmosphere.

'In the Babylon of the disorderly recovery of works of art impregnated with mud and water, every contribution ought to have been appreciated even if it was not timely. Right from the start overbearing attitudes paralysed meetings and steered us off the right track. It would be nice to gather evidence of these weaknesses but I suppose now it is no use to establish responsibilities.'

I asked Leonetto about his favourite artists.

'The period I prefer is the fourteenth century,' he said. 'It was Giotto who introduced me to the supreme pleasure of great simplicity. The Siennese school embellished their paintings with decorative patterns in bright colours which I am not so fond of. And I like the Renaissance painters even less because they took a fairly servile attitude towards authority if it was going to make them rich. I got to the point where I almost hated Leonardo da Vinci, not for his paintings, because he was a great painter, but because he kowtowed to the powerful people of his day.

'If Leonardo had had the means, he would have built an atomic bomb for the armies of the Sforza family, the rulers of Milan. He gave them new designs for weapons and he wasn't like today's scientists who design them in the hope that they are never going to be used in war. He made them expressly for destruction in order to conquer and subjugate the people.

'As a man he was extremely proud. That is clear to me even in his science. He would have liked to have invented everything and done everything and that does not imbue him with great human qualities in my eyes.'

Now that he is at the end of his career as a restorer, Leonetto has no doubts as to the value of what he has accomplished in the face of so many frustrations.

'I believe that the preservation of frescoes is important both for the history of painting and for the history of how people lived in those days. In these picture cycles, what's important is the strength of the religion and the culture. The pictures tell the story of the life, the aspirations, the faith, and the weaknesses of the people of that time. In general they renew modern man's awareness of his world. These frescoes make history tangible. You can see all the weaknesses of human nature, the vices, the greed, and also the feminine wiles of the day.'

Now, after a lifetime of suffering the agonies of seeing deteriorating masterpieces, Leonetto Tintori has had enough. 'I can't bear any more to be with stuff that's decomposing,' he said. 'It's like watching a corpse rotting away.'

For the past ten years he has been devoting himself more and more to his own artistic field – enamelled terracotta sculpture which he fires in his own kiln in the garden. He has left his own monuments to posterity to enable it to judge our age, just as he looks back on the past through the eyes of Giotto. Two of his works have been acquired by the village of Figline in whose territory he has his villa on the outskirts of Prato. One is an unconventional crucifixion scene in which an ordinary Tuscan family stands around the empty cross after the dead Christ has been removed; the other is equally imaginative – a memorial to twenty-nine villagers hanged by the retreating Nazis as a reprisal for guerilla activities. It stands near the actual oak beam which served as the gallows and shows the body of the last victim being cut down. The simplicity of Giotto has been transmitted onwards to future generations through the eyes and the hands of Leonetto Tintori.

The next generation of restorers is going to need more scientific back-up, as Leonetto indicated. One of the scientists likely to provide it is a Florentine in his thirties who operates from a laboratory and studio perched high above the roofs of his native city looking down on the Piazza della Signoria. Maurizio Seracini was trained as a doctor, went to the United States to qualify as a biochemist but found when he came home there was no hospital job for him. So he turned his attention to diagnosing sick works of art, adapting his medical knowledge to an uncharted field

He has developed mobile sonar equipment which can 'see' behind the façades of ancient buildings and reveal the successive stages of construction without picking off a single piece of plaster or removing a brick. His latest work has been the application of X-ray reflectography to paintings by Raphael, during restoration and cleaning carried out for an exhibition celebrating the five hundredth anniversary of the painter's birth. This revealed Raphael's original sketches for the paintings hidden under the surface of the paint – a development of the greatest interest to art historians which no one had considered possible until now.

'No doctor would dream of carrying out the diagnosis of a patient and no surgeon would dream of operating without first carrying out extensive tests to determine exactly what conditions he is dealing with,' Maurizio told me.

'Yet it has only been within the past year or two that the authorities here have finally been prepared to admit that the scientist has a role to play in a field which has hitherto been the exclusive preserve of the "expert" whose opinion may be important, but remains only an opinion, while I deal only with scientifically verifiable facts.

'It has always amazed me that the field of art is the only one where people are apparently prepared to hand over millions of pounds or dollars for an object whose authenticity depends on the signature of an "expert" who stands to benefit financially from his declaration. Even that doyen of Florentine art pundits, the late Bernard Berenson, did not hesitate to take his percentage from a master dealer like Duveen when paintings were being snapped up across the Atlantic during the formation of the great American art collections.

'The whole of nineteenth-century and early twentieth-century art history has to be rewritten in the light of modern knowledge which enables the dating and attribution of paintings to be carried out with scientific certainty. How many false attributions there are in the world's museums and picture galleries we shall never know, but no curator could dare pronounce today without at least a cursory scientific examination.

'Unfortunately there are few art experts around today of the stature of Leonetto Tintori. It is a poor reflection on the Italian art scene that he is better known abroad, particularly in America, than he is here.

'The world of art in Italy is controlled by two classes of people, neither of which, with rare exceptions, really care about our heritage except in so far as it affects their personal status or fortune. I refer first to the superintendents of antiquities, and their civil servant colleagues, and secondly to the antique dealers. You have no idea how these latter gentlemen manage to doll up the ware you see being delivered every year to the antique dealers' fair in Florence, highlight it with spots or bathe it in soft diffused light, surround it with velvet hangings, all to create a desire to buy which has nothing at all to do with the intrinsic value of the work of art or even its authenticity.'

I told Maurizio that I supposed he found it difficult not to get involved in local politics in working so closely with local government in Florence.

'I have always tried to steer clear of politics because I am interested in doing my job professionally,' he replied. 'But sometimes it is impossible to avoid.

'However, after years of banging at doors and of working without pay just to try and prove my point – that sick works of art need scientific diagnosis – the superintendents are finally beginning to come to me to ask for tests before carrying out significant restoration. Only at the last minute was I asked to examine the eighteen paintings by Raphael in Florence which form the centrepiece of the anniversary exhibition and which had to be cleaned rather hastily. And I only heard about the plans to restore Botticelli's *Primavera* by pure chance.

'I can't tell you how moving it is to be with these paintings day after day while you are working on them. They become your friends, and the artist, no matter how many hundreds of years ago he was born, becomes your intimate.'

Even Maurizio, the American-trained biochemist turned art restorer has been hooked by beauty.

Certain works of art in Italy seem to have such an eternal value in the eyes even of those who know or care very little about painting, that nothing, neither damage nor decay, nor even lack of visibility due to restoration work mars their perennial attraction. Such a work is Leonardo da Vinci's fresco of the Last Supper completed in the late 1490s, described as 'half-ruined' in the following century, most likely through Leonardo's own faulty technique, repainted at least six times, often by incompetent artists, vandalised by French soldiers during Napoleon's occupation of Milan, damaged by a Second World War bomb. Up to a million people every year still flock to see what's left of the painting inside the former monastery refectory adjoining the church of Santa Maria delle Grazie in Milan, where most days you will see perched on the scaffolding which obscures most of Leonardo's work a tall, blonde, middle-aged Italian woman seated, scalpel and paintbrush in hand, in front of a complicated looking microscope.

Her name is Pinin Brambilla and she has already been working for seven years upon what must surely be the most difficult art restoration project ever undertaken in Italy. Square inch by square inch she is picking the flaking surface clean, removing layers of dirt and paint before she gets down to Leonardo's original pigment. Using her specially designed Swiss-built microscope, which illuminates a tiny area and magnifies it up to forty times, she then applies solvents with the delicacy of a surgeon performing an operation, blotting them away before they destroy Leonardo's work as well. It demands immense powers of concentration and she is clearly feeling the strain. 'Last year I developed neuritis,' she told me, 'and my neck and arm get very tired as sometimes I spend up to eight hours at a stretch in front of the Last Supper.'

While Pinin Brambilla showed me the faces of Christ's Apostles that she had recovered so far from their previous piteous state, scores of Italian schoolchildren filled the refectory, joining the dozens of foreign tourists standing in admiration before what can only be described as a noble wreck. I pointed out that the dust and humidity changes caused by the coming and going of so many visitors without any system of air conditioning or humidity control could hardly be good for the fresco. She shrugged her shoulders. 'I am afraid there is indifference in my own country to these matters. But I was moved to tears by the ovation I received when I went to address a learned gathering in Washington about my work here. And every week I receive letters from art students in Britain, Canada and the United States asking if they can come and help me to restore the Leonardo. One of them even wrote that he didn't need a bed as he had a sleeping bag, and would be quite prepared simply to do the cooking.

'We still do not understand properly Leonardo's technique in this painting,' she said. 'It is a terrible weight to carry on one's shoulders, as a restorer can easily destroy a work of art even though he or she does everything according to the book.'

I left Pinin Brambilla to her labours, which she thinks will last for at least another five years, to look at another temple of the visual arts in a very different setting, the Milan Trade Fair.

Twice a year Italian fashion designers show off their collections of women's fashions to buyers from all over the world at an event that has harnessed the Italian flair for colour and design to a booming international market-place. The world of haute couture as it used to exist, dominated by Paris, has been succeeded by a brash new ready-to-wear trade in which the 'Made in Italy' tag has proved an enormous success. For five days over thirty top designers show off their wares at a series of fast-moving parades of model girls draped with what the designers believe, or rather hope, will be what every successful executive's wife in Tokyo, Frankfurt or Minneapolis will want to be seen wearing next season.

Billions of lire are spent to impress the devotees of the ready-to-wear rites. Gianni Versace, one of the new high priests of fashion opened up a shop in New York with a party for fifteen hundred guests, including many top names from international show business. Trussardi built a huge plastic dome in front of Milan cathedral to display his latest designs. The two thousand seats were so hotly contested that there were some undignified scenes of pushing and shoving as hundreds of Milan and Rome socialites tried to get inside.

The cult of beauty is taken very seriously indeed by the Italian fashion designers, who work themselves up to a high pitch of frenzy just before their show is unveiled to a well-padded audience of buyers, critics, journalists, competitors, and boutique owners from faraway places. The mannequins (mainly Americans, as Italian girls are not usually considered lanky enough, or professional enough) stand by their dressers and the clothes they will be modelling like horses at the starting post. Photographers line the catwalk

Opposite Tuscany: After the corn is cut. Pienza

Newly-weds in the rain. Boboli Gardens, Florence

Leonetto Tintori's sculpture (*above* and *opposite*) is inspired by the Tuscan countryside where he has always lived. He turned back to his first love, sculpture, when he retired from his job as a restorer of frescos. He sculpts in terracotta which he then glazes in his own kiln

Leonetto's sculpture gives him new artistic satisfaction in his retirement

Left After a lifetime devoted to restoring the works of great fresco painters of the past, Leonetto has built his own tomb in the form of a giant Noah's Ark in his garden. It is decorated with allegorical scenes of the Flood and inside are caskets for his ashes and those of his wife Elena. *Right* Leonetto and Elena – a lifetime partnership in the arts. Elena paints and her passion is her garden

Opposite Cremona: Francesco Bissolotti, a master lute maker in Stradivarius' town, carries on the ancient tradition of the craftsman

Mirella D'Angelo began her career as an international model, and she is now trying to establish herself as an actress in the depressed world of the Italian film industry. Mirella poses on one of the two oldest bridges across the River Tiber in Rome (*above* and *below left*), and (*below right*) outside the church of Saint Bartholomew on the island in the Tiber

Opposite Rome: The Colosseum. Romans have a close visual relationship with their past history

massed lens to lens. The performance takes place to the accompaniment of ear-splitting mid-Atlantic pop.

The designers all seem conscious of the fragility of the glossy-magazine world which is their creation, but it remains none the less very big business indeed. Italy's foreign currency earnings from textile exports cover the whole of her trade deficit on food imports plus part of the energy bill. The industry employs almost a quarter-of-a-million workers, mostly female.

The high priestess is undoubtedly an Italian now in her fifties called Mariuccia Mandelli, founder of the fashion empire, Krizia (she stole the name from Plato). At a meeting with other fashion designers she explained the basic insecurity surrounding the industry, notwithstanding the fact that she is building a new skyscraper headquarters for her business right in the centre of Milan.

'You are always looking at the future in the fashion world – there is always a risk of being an industry with a great future behind it.

'You have to know how to combine flair and imagination with technical knowhow. The designer has to select and identify his user very carefully. His work is based not upon the logic of production, but upon the logic of consumption of a post-industrial society. The car manufacturers understood this. That's why they now produce dozens of variations on an unchanging basic design.'

Another leading designer, Gianfranco Ferré, said he disagreed with the search for mass markets. 'The élite end of the market gives the impetus for the rest of the market. Italian designers must concentrate on identifiable quality. It's useless to waste time and effort upon mass production of cheap products. We must concentrate on the élite.'

You will get little change from a thousand dollars for any of Krizia's or Ferré's creations so there seems to be little fear for the moment of their designs getting directly into the hands of a mass market. However there is an army of copiers waiting in the wings to watch the big names and reproduce their fabrics, designs and style for foreign and domestic clients who cannot afford élite prices.

Mario Valentino from Naples is another wildly successful designer and manufacturer. He specialises in substituting leather for ordinary fabrics. Using the expertise of the old-established glove industry in Naples, he has succeeded in the space of only ten years in creating a world-wide trading organisation with branches in New York, Paris, Hong Kong, and Singapore as well as Milan and Florence.

'We still do everything by hand,' he told me, 'and never produce more than a hundred copies of the same design.'

His factory, in one of the most decrepit parts of Naples, employs over five hundred women workers, but it is still essentially a family concern, and will remain that way.

Opposite Mirella D'Angelo reflects on her acting prospects

'The secret lies in the suppleness of the leather which comes from a special cross-breed of sheep from Sardinia. We do the tanning and dyeing ourselves and I employ other designers like Versace to create new models to be sold under my name. Our factory is like a great tailor's shop.'

Inside the tailor's shop leather is sliced into long thin strips like spaghetti and woven into fabrics, pleated, plaited and folded, and coloured every conceivable hue. There is little waste. What's left over from the skins used for larger garments is used for handbags, shoes, belts and gloves. Eighty per cent of his production is exported. For all his modesty, Mario Valentino, and his wife and two sons and a daughter, are now dollar millionaires.

The Italian media do not quite know yet how to deal with the sudden international take-off of their fashion design industry. Blanket television coverage was arranged for the latest Milan collections, but commentators and public seemed unsure whether they were meant to be watching an aesthetic or a sporting event, or indeed whether it was not just one long commercial.

One big textile group decided to suspend all television publicity for a year to avoid 'damaging a product called elegance that demands discretion, good taste and reflection'.

The newspaper *La Repubblica* commented: 'television impoverishes fashion shows. The fashion designers are the new stars and television reveals their weaknesses and their fears. Those in charge of the fashion business ought to restrain themselves from showing off if they don't want to alienate the viewers. And they could begin by avoiding throwing money away on promotional banquets thronged with the wives of politicians, singers, football stars, and local government chiefs, who then complain about the cold, the bad food, the vulgarity of the proceedings and the bad company.'

Francesco Alberoni, a leading Italian sociologist, had this to say: 'Italian taste is no longer only a combination of materials, colour and design. It tries to appear as a new art form, a new *savoir-vivre*, a new form of social relations. The great fashion designers feel more and more a part of the world of show business, together with famous actors and directors.

' "Made in Italy" has now set out to conquer the United States. It is a real cultural invasion. It is using a series of elements rooted in our traditions; the figurative arts, imagination, a taste for spectacle, the Baroque, even the improvisation of the *commedia dell'arte*. In the industrial world it has chosen the most lightweight sector which borders on the field of illusion.

'The magnificence of the new merchant princes also has to hide their humble origins, to make people forget that only twenty years ago our emigrants were leaving with baggage which consisted of cardboard boxes tied together with string. It makes an impression in the great industrial cities of the West to gaze on these splendid chariots of Thespis, observing them from the ghettoes of the old emigration. Old people who have saved all their lives, who still belong to a peasant culture and remember what it is to be hungry, observe the beautiful black or white model girls, and the frantic managers and businessmen and the journalists speaking English or Italian with a Roman or Milanese accent, and they are amazed.

'These are two different worlds at the opposite ends of the spectrum. And yet they have something in common. That old man with rough hands is ashamed of his poverty, but he is also ashamed at the histrionic, frivolous character of the New Wave. Because it reminds him of the art of survival and he recognises something false about it. And the *nouveau riche*, the refined seller of fashions, knows that the older man knows, and feels insecure.

'When you come down to it, they are two different generations of migrants looking for recognition and legitimacy in a difficult, hostile world.'

The passion for design has recently hit an industry which at first sight has little need for the services of an industrial designer, except perhaps in the packaging of the product. Mario Nervegna, the managing director of the Voiello spaghetti factory in Naples, decided that, as his company had not changed the shapes of pasta that it manufactured since the nineteenth century, it was about time for something new to tempt palates and to boost sales. So he engaged the services of Giorgetto Giugiaro, a top industrial designer from Turin in the north who is more at home creating aerodynamic shapes for new motor cars (twelve million production models based on his designs are on the roads) rather than plates of spaghetti.

Giugiaro's response was enthusiastic. 'I love pasta,' he admitted, so he set to work at his drawing board with an elaborate specification from Mario Nervegna. He had to produce a shape that was palatable, absorbed flavour easily, had sufficient elasticity when you bit it, did not break into small pieces when in a dry state, was compatible with different types of sauces, and finally had to look good.

'The problem was,' Giugiaro said, 'were we to follow tradition, or to make an evocative, futuristic shape, symbolic of our time?

'I didn't ask for advice from housewives. I design for myself and asked myself the question, what sort of shape do I prefer?

'The design I came up with fits easily into the plate unlike ordinary spaghetti which knits itself into a heap.'

'Food should be arranged on the plate in an aesthetic orderly fashion, as the Japanese do, and not left higgledy-piggledy.'

Giugiaro speaks from experience about the qualities of industrial design appreciated in Japan, as he has produced designs for some of the biggest Japanese manufacturers of watches, reflex cameras, and cosmetics.

'We Italians have this age-old desire to add something personal to what nature has created,' he went on. 'We are unsatisfied individualists. We always want to retouch and to improve. I know things can be beautiful without refining

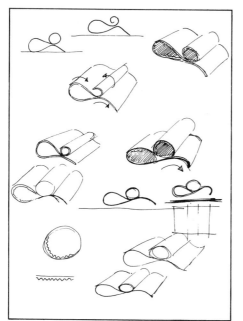

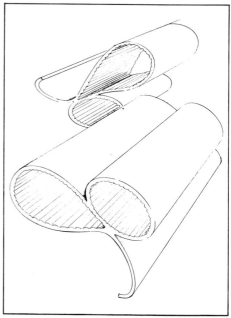

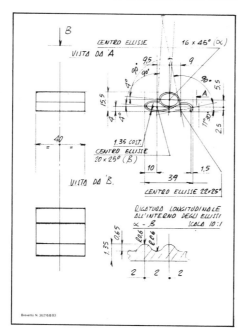

Giorgetto Giugiaro and his elegant designs for a new form of pasta

them constantly, and it may be rather a presumptuous attitude, but this is our special quality.'

Custom-built spaghetti turned out to be a wild success. The final result of Giugiaro's drawings, four mock-ups, much tasting and comparing of notes was a creation which resembles the double helix and which was named 'Marille'.

100 *Italians*

Mario Nervegna explained why. 'Some people thought the new shape looked like a marriage between two pieces of maccheroni and a lasagne. Others thought it looked like a butterfly or a flower. Yet others saw the shape of the Greek letter Beta, and one taster said it reminded him of the waves of the sea. So we called it Marille after *"mare"* which means the sea in Italian.

'One consideration was that it had to be suitable for diet-conscious consumers. Eight pieces weigh only fifty grammes and that cannot make you fat. A plateful of Marille only contains half the quantity by weight of pasta that you get in a plateful of spaghetti.'

The launching of designer-spaghetti was a commercial as well as an aesthetic success. Production is as yet limited and demand, particularly in Northern Italy, has been so great that it is often being sold under the counter, a rare event in food-conscious Italy.

SEVEN

Pasta and Circuses

> *Trahit sua quemque voluptas.*
> Everyone is dragged on by his favourite pleasure.
>
> Virgil (died Brindisi 19 BC)

During the 1970s, the Italians did a most uncharacteristic thing. In the name of the new God, economic efficiency, who is reputed to lack followers in their country, they abolished several public holidays observed for many generations in the calendar of the Roman Catholic Church.

Thus the Epiphany (6 January) and the Corpus Domini (24 June) were among the days struck off the list of seventeen officially recognised holidays which until then had given Italy the distinction of leading the world in matters of time off.

The art of the '*ponte*', or making a 'bridge' between a public holiday and the preceding or following weekend in order to create a longer break, had been refined in Italy to the point that for at least a week in most months of the year, quite apart from the 'dead' holiday months of July and August, work came to a halt in most government offices.

In Italy the pleasure ethic has always tended to dominate the work ethic. The Roman emperors used to vie with their predecessors in the number and length of holidays they granted for public games and festivals, until the confused and contented populace of Rome lost count of which days they were actually supposed to be working.

So it is not surprising that modern Italians should have shown ability in the organisation of leisure both for themselves, in their newly affluent society, and for the foreign hordes from all over the world who descend each year upon their shores.

On any given night Italy has more beds available for visitors than any other country in the world, except the United States. With its 41,000 classified hotels, and many thousands more modest establishments and camping sites, Italy can sleep up to four million holidaymakers and business visitors.

Four out of five families take their annual holidays in July or August. Only five per cent go outside Italy. The favourite destination is France, followed by Yugoslavia.

Nearly half the population spend their holidays with relations or friends, or in their second home, one person in ten goes camping, and two in ten stay in hotels or in rented accommodation.

The great magnet is the sea, and particularly the eight hundred miles of wide sandy Adriatic beaches with their safe bathing, all the way from Trieste in the north to Brindisi in the south. A quarter of all Italian holidaymakers find their way there during the summer. The most successful, and the biggest resort, in fact the biggest seaside resort now in all Europe, is Rimini. Organised sea bathing began there in the mid-nineteenth century, and by 1930 Rimini had become a smart international resort, dominated by its Grand Hotel, now alas only a shadow of its former magnificence. The activities there of the wealthy and the famous were observed by the young Federico Fellini, the film director, who was born in Rimini. He let his imagination run riot about the scene later in his film *Amarcord*, a biographical fantasy. His memories are vivid, fifty years on.

'On summer evenings the Grand Hotel became to us Istanbul, Baghdad, Hollywood,' Fellini said. 'We boys ran around like so many mice gaping at those brilliant salons, where beautiful women and men in dinner jackets were living the lives of the Ziegfeld follies.

'Then,' Fellini remembered, 'we went round the back of the hotel where you could see all those beautiful shining motor cars: the Isotta Fraschinis, the Bugattis, the Mercedes Benz. The chauffeurs, with their polished boots, lit cigarettes as they waited and walked their masters' and mistresses' pet dogs, nasty aggressive little creatures, on a leash. You could hear the strains of American songs like 'Sonny Boy' reverberating in the air. In our imagination the Grand Hotel was the scene of passion, crime and international intrigue.

'For me the Grand Hotel remains a fabulous place of decadent luxury, of oriental splendour. I don't recognise my city Rimini any more. There used to be miles of dark around the city and just one street along the sea shore. Now there's no more darkness, just ten miles of night clubs and flashing neon signs. One fabulous disco after another, you don't see anything like them, even in Las Vegas.

'I go back to Rimini less and less. I feel cheated. A city that I had stored away in my memory in a certain way, has become a giant, it is a city that has grown without consulting me, without asking my permission. I would like to ask all those folk there, the Germans, the Swedes, the young people from Milan and Rome: "What on earth do you find so attractive here? What have you come here for?"'

The answer to Federico Fellini's question could be supplied by any of the millions of visitors, three-quarters of them Italians, who throng Rimini's wide beaches for four months each year: sun, sand and sex.

The sun factory is a very big business indeed. The hotels off the Adriatic coast over seven thousand of them, make an annual net profit of over £250 million and most of them are small family run affairs. They work flat out between June and September, are empty for most of the rest of the year, but allow their owners to live a life of ease for the eight months' pause between Rimini seasons.

Italian beaches are by law free and open to all. It costs nothing to dip your toes in the sea or walk along the shoreline. But if you want to sit down, erect an umbrella, or stretch out on the sand in Rimini, you will inevitably come into contact with the man who presides over all the daily rituals of the beach, the *bagnino*, or beach-master.

The *bagnini* of Rimini got together in 1972 and formed a co-operative to exploit their concessions granted by the local council. In exchange for an annual fee, they gained the right to charge for the hire of beach huts, sunbeds, umbrellas, deckchairs, and sundry other equipment now considered indispensable by Italian holidaymakers at the seaside. The rates in 1984 were the lira equivalent of about one hundred pounds a month for enough gear for a family of three, umbrella and beach hut included.

Claudio Casadei is the king of sea-front concession number 72, forty yards of sand filled with fifteen rows of gaily coloured sunshades. His badge of authority is a peaked naval-type white cap. Claudio, grizzled but clearly hale at sixty-four, explained to me that he started from nothing after Rimini was practically flattened by RAF bombs in World War Two.

'After the war we cleaned up the beach, removed all the military debris and gradually tourism took off. In 1964 there were some disastrous floods which swept everything away, once again. Then the sunbed took over from the deckchair.

'At the start I had just two sunbeds. Nobody wanted them, so I found a couple of pretty girls, and said: "You can lie there for nothing if you like."

'Suddenly it began to take off. Now we have six hundred sunbeds and there are never enough of them, you can see.

'We made a conscious decision – tourism for the masses at a reasonable price, not tourism for an élite. If we had catered for an élite, like Fellini's Grand Hotel crowd, we would never have been able to provide jobs for everyone around here. In the mountains around Rimini people were very poor indeed.'

The tourist trade now gives lucrative seasonal employment to a quarter of the population of Rimini and its hinterland. The whole Casadei family takes part in the beach business, Claudio and his wife Prima, who cooks for the rest of the family in the beach cabin which becomes office, kitchen and dining room for them during the summer, his son Giancarlo and daughter-in-law Elisabeta, and their children, plus sundry cousins. They are up to ten for lunch and dinner around the beach hut table.

Claudio told me how the *bagnino* has gone up in the local social pecking order since it became such a profitable trade. He takes an average £600 a day, just in beach gear rentals, between June and September.

'The *bagnino* has become someone who counts here. He isn't considered a manual worker any more. He's there to give advice, help anyone who feels unwell, or gets into difficulty in the sea. You have to know how to carry out life-saving, the kiss of life for drowning accidents, how to deal with fainting and lost children.

'I see myself as an important person because I bring order with me wherever I go. If people are playing around with a football, they stop it straight away when I arrive. I don't accept people stepping on my toes. I come from Romagna[1] and have character, you know. I have always lived close to the sea, where you learn to be level-headed, otherwise you don't survive. I am very polite, I never raise my voice. But my words count for more than those that are shouted.'

Claudio prefers Italians to other nationalities on his patch of beach because of their free-spending habits on holiday. Whatever money they have got, they spend, and that's it. The Italians don't calculate when they're on holiday.'

His son Giancarlo, who took over the business side from Claudio when his father reached sixty, said he found the British good clients both for the sunbeds and the bar, particularly the bar. 'They may drink their tea at five in the afternoon, but they also patronise the bar all day long.' (There was an eleven per cent increase in British tourist arrivals in Rimini in 1983.)

Giancarlo said he found the Germans 'rather calculating'.

The Rimini beach day follows a strict timetable, signalled by the frequent raising and lowering of coloured flags. 'Up till nine-thirty in the morning the red and yellow flag flies which means there is no lifeguard service,' Giancarlo explained. 'Next the yellow goes up, if it's fine weather, and finally at ten minutes past ten when everyone has arrived at work, the white flag.

'At a quarter-past-twelve the yellow flag goes up again as the lifeguards take their lunch break. White flag at three-fifteen, which stays up until five minutes to six and then back to red and yellow at six-thirty. If the weather is bad the red flag stays up all day.'

The serried ranks of umbrellas and the booming beach trade make it difficult to imagine what it was all like forty years ago when Giancarlo's father, Claudio, began working on the sands, as an alternative to being a fisherman.

'There were great private villas beside the hotels and the owners would have an umbrella or two, or moveable screens or curtains to shade their guests from the sun. We *bagnini* acted as their workforce, doing stupid things like shifting the screens around according to the position of the sun. But slowly, slowly their authority was undermined and we eventually stopped doing such simple-minded work.

'Then there were the hotels with thirty or forty rooms and only three screens on the beach. The guests used to have to race to get a place in the shade every morning. It's much better now.

1. The region which, as the tourist brochures remind visitors, also gave birth to Mussolini, Toscanini, Verdi and Marconi.

'We have to spend a lot on cleaning the beach every morning. The lorries set out at five in the morning. If there's been a storm and the beach is covered with seaweed we have mechanical scrapers. By half-past seven, the sand is always clean and raked.'

Cousin Rina runs the café-bar on Claudio's beach. She serves toasted sandwiches, pizza, ice cream, tea, coffee, beer, or harder liquor, and sometimes has trouble with foreigners demanding exotic sounding cocktails. She seems to be on nodding acquaintance with every other passer-by and, like the rest of the Casadei family, stays at Claudio's beach from early morning till late at night. 'It's very hard work,' she said, 'but in the winter we live like lords.'

Dress, on Claudio's beach, is optional, provided you retain the minimum. Topless bathing has become commonplace in the Italy of the eighties, after years of rearguard action by southern magistrates outraged at what they considered the shameless exposure of sun-starved, liberated northern woman.

As usual in Italy, the aesthetics get mixed up with traditional morals. In 1982 the mayor of Tropea, a small seaside resort in Calabria, issued a local ordinance banning topless bathing except by young girls and what he described as 'attractive women'. A storm broke out when the local council tried to define an 'attractive woman' and the ordinance was cancelled. Later the same year Giovanni Petrillo the Christian Democrat mayor of the island of Pantelleria, Italy's southernmost Mediterranean outpost, poised not far from the coast of North Africa and a paradise for nudists, posted a ban on nude bathing in which he let his feelings run away with him.

The mayor deplored, in large print, 'the lamentable, scandalous behaviour of some women who expose to the sun breasts that resemble extended, flaccid, fleshy excrescences, more like extra stomachs than anything else . . .'

In local elections in Trieste in 1983, a radical party candidate, Dora Petrilli (a thirty-six-year-old teacher with a passion for nude sunbathing, no relation to the mayor of Pantelleria) held her election meetings in a state of nature in order to draw attention to her conflict with the law.

Neither Claudio, nor Giancarlo are affected by the topless parade on their beach.

'When it first started,' Giancarlo said, 'everyone from young boys to grandparents used to go down on the promenade to watch the topless girls. If the girls are young, they are good to look at, full stop. But unfortunately, most of them are getting on a bit, so there's nothing to get excited about.

'I prefer a woman with a beautiful split on the thigh, up to here perhaps,' he said, motioning with his hand. 'That gives you more to imagine. I personally don't go much for half-naked women.'

Giancarlo does not allow his sixteen-year-old daughter Cristina to go topless.

Claudio said: 'I like women dressed, not naked. I can undress them myself. I don't like women who are already undressed. It's not beautiful. It's like being in

Africa or India. It becomes a primitive way of life. There's no longer real sexual attraction between men and women. You can look at all the topless girls but it quickly becomes boring. You can look at beautiful things in a shop window, can't you?'

There is an unspoken sexual code about where you sit on the Rimini beach. The closer you are to the sea, the more open you are to offers. Families almost always sit in the 'safe' area under the umbrellas close to the *bagnino's* hut. Those who might be interested, if the right person came along, lie on sunbeds near the shore, while those who are definitely available sit near the water's edge or actually in the sea.

At night, the beach is dotted with courting couples. This is the second or third stage in the boy-meets-girl sequence; the first occurs when there is an approach on the beach during the day and he asks her if she would like a trip on a *moscone*. The *moscone* comes in two types, with pedals or oars. Both achieve the same aim of isolating the girl from the shore, and at the same time half-scaring her to death so that she turns to her gallant oarsmen or pedal-man for protection. What happens next can be snapped by any camera with a long lens.

The *passeggiata*, the late afternoon street parade which can be witnessed in any small Italian town when the locals go out to see and be seen, look at the shops, dawdle, and transact their affairs, has naturally been transferred to the beaches. Both men and women tend to walk around with their stomach muscles pulled in for their daily speculative tour of what's on display.

The *passeggiata* also gives an opportunity to the young to escape from the entire family circle who have most likely accompanied them to the beach.

Every shape and size of human kind is on display on Rimini's beaches in variegated shades of red, white and brown, laid out under the watchful eye of the *bagnino* and the less than watchful eye of the *salvataggio* or lifeguard who may very well have gone off for a little *passeggiata* of his own to some other part of the sands. Luckily the gradually sloping shore means that bathing is extremely safe along this part of the Adriatic coast, and few people drown.

The beach displays a high degree of organisation for Italy, and new arrivals, particularly those from abroad, often wander around dazed at first. Usually they sit down on the first empty seat they find, which happens to belong to the *bagnino*.

Everything is laid out precisely in rows on the perfectly flat sands; for miles and miles along the coast in both directions the scene is the same. Hence the large number of lost toddlers usually speedily united with their families by means of a blaring beach-wide public address system.

Guaranteed sunshine (it rains on average in Rimini only twenty-six days during the entire summer, and rarely for more than an hour or two at a stretch) is the main reason for Rimini's success, apart from the shrewdness and enterprise of the people who run this vast holiday hypermarket.

Many of them, like Giancarlo, have not merely got to know foreign girls there, but married them. He first met his blonde wife Elisabeta, who comes from Norway, when she spent a fortnight's holiday in Rimini in 1964 at the age of seventeen.

She admitted that her ideas about Italians had changed somewhat since then.

'When I went to school we used to think the Italian mamma was a big fat woman with fifteen children, dressed in black and a black shawl round her head. But when I arrived here it was quite different. People in Rimini are much more modern than those in the south. Italians are much warmer and romantic than Norwegians.

'I don't give Giancarlo too much freedom however. If he feels like going out on the town, I tell him I am coming too. I'm not like Italian women who say yes, all right, and then he'll come home with a bunch of flowers next morning. No, that doesn't work for me!'

Every conceivable form of popular entertainment is available for the holiday masses in Rimini once the sun has gone down and the beaches have been taken over by couples enjoying more isolated pleasures than those available during the daylight hours. Cinemas, indoor and outdoor, video-news from home, if you are a foreigner, talent shows, strip joints, beauty contests, old-time dancing, hundreds of seafood restaurants, bars, ice-cream parlours, shops open till all hours, an illuminated Italy in miniature, complete with scale models of the Alps, the Colosseum and Milan Cathedral, nothing more than three feet high, video games galore, mud baths, rock-concerts, recitals, dozens and dozens of discos including one of the biggest in Europe called *L'Altro Mondo* (the Other World) constructed like a space ship with a DJ console that sinks and then rises into the roof, go-go dancers in lighted tubes around the ceiling and a huge illuminated dance floor, and a reptile house, open till midnight, where the jaded can experience the thrill of seeing poisonous rattlesnakes wearily killing live hamsters which gambol in front of the snakes' cages unaware of their impending doom.

In winter, practically all the hotels and *pensioni*, the boarding houses, are closed, the discos are shuttered, the beach deserted, empty even of umbrellas. The summer crowds seem unimaginable, a mirage. Claudio and his family, after taking long holidays themselves, return to varnish and repair their beach furniture, do a little fishing, plan for next season. In the nearby resort of Riccione however, the go-ahead Communist mayor, Terzo Pierani, dreams of the day when the tourist season might last for twelve months in the year.

He has closed off the main street, brought in truckloads of sand from the beach, put up the umbrellas outside the cafés, notwithstanding the bitter cold, populated the artificial summer with plastic shop-window models, draped in bikinis. Nobody is taken in, but one hardy soul insists on sitting out in a deckchair and is served his Campari bitter by a waiter draped in a thick winter scarf. The mayor has organised dancing in the streets for New Year's Eve, and Rimini next door has countered with a Fancy Dress Ball aimed at attracting a more exclusive crowd, with guests dressed up in thirties and forties style as in the days of Fellini's memories of the Grand Hotel.

There's a congress of palaeontologists and a new archaeological museum to see, and you can have an excellent fish meal with the local white wine at any time of year. There's golf, a casino, and an ice-rink, all in full swing. And there are even a few people walking along the beach, although they are easily outnumbered by the seagulls. The shops are allowed to open on Sundays if they want. Only the sun is missing.

As a nation, the Italians may be individualists, but they are also gregarious by habit and like to follow the crowd in their leisure and pleasure. Basically they have a very traditional and conservative attitude to life, and are as loth to change their eating habits, as they are to change the period when they take their holidays, or the political parties they vote for.

Fresh green vegetables and fruit are as essential a part of the average Italian's diet, and have been for generations, as the ubiquitous pasta in any of its myriad shapes. Italian migrants have taken their food habits to other parts of the world and have even caused changes in their host country's diet. Before the influx of Italians into Toronto and Quebec in Canada in the fifties and sixties, there was a scarcity of fresh fruit and vegetables on sale there during the hard winter. Now fresh supplies are flown in daily from the warmer climes of California, and they are tastefully arranged Italian-style in the greengrocers' shops all the year round.

Naples, now famous for its pasta, used to be renowned for its green leaf vegetables. Until the eighteenth century the staple food there was cabbage, spinach and meat.

It has been calculated from local slaughterhouse records in Naples that in 1563 a cow was slaughtered for every ten inhabitants, a calf for every 22, and a goat for every 18. Taking into account the tripling of the population by the mid-twentieth century, the figures had gone down four centuries later to one cow for every 97 Neapolitans, a sheep for every 920, and a calf for every 29. This admittedly rough comparison shows how meat-eating declined, not so much because of the increase in pasta consumption, but because of the steady impoverishment of the population which led to the abandonment of more costly and nutritious food habits.

The invention of the pasta press in Naples during the eighteenth century undoubtedly helped the spaghetti boom. (President Thomas Jefferson introduced the spaghetti press into America in 1789.) But even the ancient Romans ate pasta. We know that the poet Horace used to have for his supper a bowl of 'lagana', today called 'lasagne', a flat pasta normally cooked in the oven with grated Parmesan cheese.

Maccheroni used to be regarded as a luxury food. It was often served as a sweet; the English 'macaroon' is derived from it, as is the French 'macaron', first mentioned in Rabelais. Late Latin texts frequently refer to lasagne.

A Latin codex dated 1338 by one Mastro Barnabà from Reggio Emilia describes the local names of various types of pasta in northern Italy. They include 'vermicelli' and 'pancadelle' (known today as 'papardelle').

So it was not until relatively recent times that Naples became the maccheroni capital of Europe. And it was not until the mid-nineteenth century that the Neapolitans began to garnish and flavour their maccheroni with tomato, instead of cheese.

Mario Nervegna, who runs five pasta factories in and around Naples producing over one hundred different shapes and squiggles apart from the classic spaghetti form, told me he regards his company as 'the Deutsche Gramophon' of the Italian pasta industry today. It was he who commissioned a top industrial designer in Turin to invent a new shape for his up-market trade.

'These distinctive shapes arose because each used to have its own taste. These differences have largely disappeared as the manufacture of food has become more standardised.

'In Italy we are in danger of losing the taste of primitive foods. We tend to treat wine in this country as if it were water, without judging its quality. The leavening of bread used to take all night, now it's done in two hours and the bread has no taste.

'Italians eat one-and-a-half-million metric tonnes of pasta every year. We only supply three per cent of that market, but we are maintaining the Neapolitan tradition of pasta making. Artisan-type production may not be competitive inside the factories, but we catch up on efficient distribution and marketing.'

There are computers and flow-charts everywhere in the offices of Mario Nervegna's pasta company; the factories are automated and very noisy but the pasta is allowed to dry very slowly in huge drying chambers in order to give it more flavour. Durum wheat, or semolina, half of it produced in Italy and half imported from Texas, is mixed with water in huge vats, then extruded into the required shape before going through the slow drying process.

The number of pasta producers in Italy has fallen heavily in recent years, mainly as a result of takeover battles by the industrial food giants. The market leader takes a hefty eighteen per cent of total sales. Mario's problem in getting a bigger share of the potential market for better quality pasta is that the Italian housewife is normally unwilling to spend a few lire more for a product such as pasta or detergents upon which she is usually looking to save money. In Naples itself he now has to sell his product at a special 'political' price, twenty per cent below that fixed for the rest of the country, in order to meet the competition in a city living in a permanent state of economic crisis.

'The different provinces of Italy have never been very wealthy, and their culture has been manifest in something very banal – their cooking. The value of the regional cuisine, quite apart from its gastronomic qualities, is shown in local literature. If we lose these values, we are losing something very precious.

'Take polenta for example. I was brought up in Udine, in the north. In that part of Italy the basic food was polenta and within the space of thirty years it has disappeared. It is a poor peasant type of food. But the fact remains that the basic foodstuff of a people which has lasted for centuries has gone. It's dramatic.

'Now the decline in pasta consumption is nothing like that; only two per cent a year at present. But eating habits are changing. The midday meal which used to be the main occasion for eating pasta is changing style. Fast food is taking over for millions. We are planning to set up fifty hamburger factories in the next five years. We are importing not only a non-native eating habit, but also the technology upon which we have to pay royalties, without giving a thought that we are witnessing a decline in the Italian style of cooking. I wouldn't like the pasta market to disappear like polenta. Twenty years ago the polenta market was worth £180 million a year. Now it's just a delicacy you can find in a few specialised restaurants.

'These changes in taste in Italy can be shattering. Look at the women's petticoat market. A friend of mine was the marketing manager of a company that only produced petticoats. Suddenly, in the late sixties, Italian women began wearing trousers. The market slumped from one week to the next. A company which was a market leader suddenly found itself without any sales. Only now, fifteen years later, is it just beginning to pick up again.'

Some Italian housewives will still never go into a shop to buy pasta in a packet. They make their own at home, as everyone did in days gone by.

Antonina Manglaviti who lives in the village of San Pantaleone on the slopes of the Aspromonte in remote Calabria would never dream of offering her family commercially produced pasta.

'We wouldn't know what we are getting to eat,' she said. 'Home-made pasta takes three hours to prepare, but time is not important. The taste is what matters, and the natural flavour.'

'What we get in shops is adulterated. Everything is genuine here,' added her husband Giuseppe, who runs a 150-acre farm on which he produces all the family's flour, olive oil and wine, not to mention their meat, milk, fruit, vegetables, cheese, and eggs.

Adelio Pagani, head chef at Rome's Grand Hotel, would agree. I went to see him in his kitchens presiding over a staff of forty-two cooks on the day he happened to be preparing lunch for King Juan Carlos of Spain, on a private visit to Italy, as well as for hotel guests.

'Italians love eating pasta,' he said, 'but it makes them fat. The secret is to mix it with foods that are not fattening and easy to digest, such as greenstuffs.

On the whole I find Italians know how to eat healthily. Garlic and onions were the antibiotics of my grandparents, and pure olive oil is my hydraulic fluid.

'At work I am tasting and nibbling all the time, and I have noticed that hotel guests like to nibble as well. So we started a help-yourself buffet in the main restaurant and it has become very popular.

'The French are perfectionists in cooking. We Italians never had anyone comparable to Escoffier who amalgamated all the best French cooking traditions into a single style. In Italy we have very creative regional cooking traditions.

'I am a gourmet, as well as a cook who likes his profession,' Adelio admitted. 'Sometimes I take off my chef's hat to enjoy the pleasures of the table myself.'

I asked him who did the cooking at home.

'My wife,' he said.

Italian families often combine an excursion into the country with culinary acquisitions. Mushroom hunting can lead to a stampede at certain times in the year in wooded areas where the prized '*porcini*' are to be found. The groups you see peering at the ground in the Roman Campagna on a Sunday afternoon are more likely to be searching for a type of dandelion leaf, delicious in salads, than for archaeological remains.

Ferruccio Berolo, a retired professional dancer, who now runs two ballet schools for children near Venice, was born and brought up at Belluno in the foothills of the Alps. There he acquired the habit of searching for herbs in the fields to flavour his cooking, a constant delight to him.

'You can perform miracles with very simple, cheap ingredients like herbs,' he said. 'Cooking for me is social, it entertains, and it is a pleasure for my nostrils, my mouth, and my stomach. I specialise in peasant type food. I grew up in the mountains, so I am used to it.

'I could write poems about food,' Ferruccio went on, warming to his subject. 'I once read some Persian poetry about aubergines. Such a joy! I could see them all shining, round, plump and sensual.

'As soon as you are born into this world you start eating, and when you come to die, they give you that famous last sip of water before you start your journey towards eternity.

'Food is the main thing; it fulfils, and it is beautiful to look at. Have you ever looked, really looked at Italian food? All that pasta, red and shining, all glossy and rich and floppy, it makes the eyes shine as well, you know.'

Ferruccio lives in a small *calle* (the Venetian name for a street) just off the Grand Canal. He described his three local bars, for which he clearly has great affection, as an extension of his living room.

'It is not a question of going there, sitting down gloomily to have a couple of sad boozes. It is like going to a friend's house; the only difference is that you pay for the drinks instead of having them free.

'You meet your friends only if you really want to. If not, you tell them straight you want to be alone.

'I have three favourite bars. I call them "the Triangle" and go from one to another. The last one I call "the Pirate Cove" as the barmen all look like pirates. The wine is good and the Triangle scene always ends up in their pub.

'Mind you, not every day. If I have a very solid day's work, maybe I have only one glass in one corner of the Triangle. I crawl to the bar and say "*Ciao*, Franco! Give me a '*prosecco*'" [a slightly fizzy white wine produced near Venice].

'There's this divine thing, cool, with tiny bubbles looking like floating pearls, and when you have it, oh God, at that point you forget everything, that's heaven, there are no two ways about it!'

EIGHT

Laugh, Clown!

> *Ridi, Pagliaccio!*
> (Laugh, Clown!)
>
> Pietro Mascagni
> *I Pagliacci*
>
> The people of Rome are probably fonder of sharp, biting satire than
> those of any other European city. Their subtle wit seizes avidly upon the
> most obscure allusions. What makes them much funnier than, say,
> Londoners, is the sheer desperation of their situation.
>   Accustomed to consider their problems as inevitable and eternal, the
> middle classes do not get angry at a Minister or wish to kill him; his
> successor would be just as bad. What the common people want above all
> is to mock the powerful and to laugh behind their backs. Because of
> severe censorship, you have to go to marionette performances to have a
> good laugh. I spent a delightful evening at the marionette show in Piazza
> Fiano . . .
>
> Stendhal
> *Travels in Italy*

To find out about contemporary Italians' sense of humour, I consulted Giorgio
Forattini, the country's leading political cartoonist. His off-the-cuff reply was
not encouraging. 'A scarce commodity,' he said.

Forattini created journalistic history in a country where politicians take
themselves very seriously indeed, by getting his cartoons published for the first
time ever on the front page of national daily newspapers. The breakthrough
came in 1974 when he was working for the Communist-oriented afternoon
newspaper *Paese-Sera*. The occasion was the Divorce Law referendum (which
resulted in a resounding 'No' in response to a proposal, supported more or less
openly by the Vatican, to abolish the newly passed bill legalising divorce).

The cartoon, admittedly not a comic masterpiece, showed a bottle of
champagne with the cork popping and the cork had the face of Amintore
Fanfani, a veteran Christian Democrat who had led the abolition campaign.
The punchline read: 'Let's celebrate, the cork's gone!'

The judgement turned out to be premature, as Fanfani returned again for a
spell as Prime Minister, but Forattini's cartoons began to become a hot property

in newspaper terms and he moved later to the front page of the rather staid anti-Communist *La Stampa*, set off by a sea of fine print. He draws instant cartoons at election time to amuse viewers of the main channel of the State television network, RAI, but he is still something of a phenomenon as he must be the only cartoonist in Italy actually earning his living from political satire. He habitually portrays one former Prime Minister, renowned for his portliness, completely naked, and another current leader dressed as a Mussolini blackshirt, and he gets away with his impertinences (see page 116).

Forattini told me he believes that Italians lack interior happiness and security and this is the reason why they laugh less than, the British. 'If they are stuck in a traffic jam for example they will hoot, make a lot of noise, or attack each other, but they will not sit back and laugh at the situation.

'An Italian will always have to face this hidden dilemma when he is faced with something funny. Can he afford to laugh?'

Italy's leading cartoonist began his career as a travelling salesman covering thousands of miles every week in his small Fiat selling car accessories and later long-playing records. But after twenty years on the road he got tired of flogging around the towns and villages of north and south and had his first cartoons published in the early seventies.

'My first strip cartoon character was called Stradivarius. He was an absent-minded travelling salesman whose hobby was playing the violin but who tried to sell mincing machines; he kept getting the boxes mixed up and brought out his violin case in front of his potential clients.

'Since I began to make a name for myself as a political satirist, the politicians have come to fear me, yet they are flattered at the same time. Giovanni Spadolini [whom Forattini portrays naked] once said on television that he owed a good part of his political success to my caricatures.

'I am a moralist. I don't practice politics, but my subject is politics. I am not simply anti-Communist, I am anti-all the political parties. That is the reason for my success.

'When I was working for *Paese-sera* I was never allowed to do cartoons of left-wingers or Communists. My first cartoon of the late Communist leader Enrico Berlinguer was inspired by his attempts to make overtures to the Catholics. I drew him giving a communion wafer to a beefy workman with a red handkerchief round his neck.

'The Italian Communists have no sense of humour. They were the ones who used to get angriest when I was working for *La Repubblica*. They used to ring up the Editor and call me an imbecile.

'The Christian Democrats are smarter. They know, even if they are boiling with rage, that they have to laugh at my drawings. The current Prime Minister, Bettino Craxi, a Socialist, gets very angry at some of my drawings, I am told, but he has never made any personal protest to me.

* Anno 116   Numero 172 *

LA STAMPA

REDAZIONE, AMMINISTRAZIONE, TIPOGRAFIA: 10126 TORINO, VIA MARENCO 32, C...

Martedì 17 Agosto

A PAGINA 3

CACCIA

Uno sport aristocratico. Mentre si apre in quasi tutte le regioni la stagione venatoria
di Ippolito Pizzetti

A PAGINA 6

GRAHAM GRE

Nizza fra angeli e pes
le polemiche dopo il «na
dello scrittore inglese
strato in Francia
di Franco

Lo sgombero dei palestinesi forse a fine settimana

E' fatta: Begin rinuncia alle liste dei «fedayn»

E' caduto anche il rifiuto d'Israele ai parà francesi: Parigi ha assicurato Gerusalemme che la ritira se l'Olp non rispetta il calendario delle partenze - Ultima condizione: i guerriglieri di Arafat devono consegnare un pilota israeliano prigioniero

DAL NOSTRO INVIATO SPECIALE

BEIRUT — Nella città squassata, ferita da due mesi di bombardamenti, e ora ritornata da quattro giorni a una quiete carica di speranze incerte, i palestinesi si preparano a partire: l'evacuazione è ormai imminente. Gli israeliani hanno rifiutato l'offerta pesante dalle alture sovrastanti Beirut Ovest, i fedayn si contano, organizzano lo sgombero, gli ufficiali americani, francesi, italiani, studiano insieme l'arrivo e lo spiegamento delle truppe e la ...ltinazionale di pace. I negoziatori stanno mettendo le virgole all'accordo, che per Sharon equivale a una «resa» palestinese, e che per Arafat è come l'inizio di un nuovo esilio dopo una «resistenza vittoriosa».

Nel convento di Sant'Antonio, dove è installato lo stato maggiore di Tsahal, un dirigente della diplomazia israeliana esprime l'improvvisa disponibilità del governo di Gerusalemme. Begin non esige più le liste dei fedayn, con l'esatta destinazione di ciascuno. Quelle liste, negate da Arafat, possono essere consegnate ai fedayn stessi. Il rifiuto della forza francese come primo contingente di pace? Gerusalemme avrebbe preferito gli italiani. Il dirigente della diplomazia israeliana lo dice chiaro e tondo. Ma al momento che Parigi offre garanzie precise (in questo senso Chryssson ha salvato a Begin) il ritiro immediato, e pure nel rispettassero il calendario delle partenze, Gerusalemme non ha più obiezioni.

In quanto ai cerimoniale della partenza, gli israeliani si non arretreranno di un passo, ma saranno invisibili. I fedayn non passeranno sotto le loro baionette, ma saranno sorvegliati. Saranno tenuti d'occhio. I soldati libanesi magari sedti tra i massimi, il controllerà in...al primo spiegamento e raccoglieranno le armi pesanti. Al porto ci potranno essere anche le truppe francesi, la Legione Straniera di Mitterrand, al momento dell'imbarco, nell'attesa di prendere posizione con gli italiani e gli americani lungo la linea di demarcazione.

In sostanza, il «piano Habib», presentato una settimana fa, che verrà applicato con tanto ritardo, e con decine di morti in più. Una sola condizione israeliana, non prevista in quel documento: la liberazione del pilota catturato dai palestinesi. E' dunque per quel prigioniero che Sharon ha fatto bombardare Beirut Ovest mercoledì e giovedì?

L'evacuazione dovrebbe cominciare sabato prossimo, forse prima, venerdì, o tutt'al più il giorno di ieri. La destinazione del primo scaglione Olp sarà Aqaba in Giordania, da raggiungere via mare, attraverso il Canale di Suez. Ad alteni

deriti in quel porto del Mar Rosso i palestinesi troveranno i beduini che nel 1970, per difendere il regno di Re Hussein, massacrarono e cacciarono i fedayn. Il sovrano ha scemita e ora disposto ad accogliere i palestinesi con passaporto giordano e ad assegnare coloro che hanno perduto la cittadinanza giordana. I fedayn ritornano, an-

mi simbolico, sul luogo di una loro tragedia, una delle tante, una delle più pesanti: il ...settembre nero: di 12 anni or sono. I senza passaporto, e sono i più, andranno via terra in Siria, dove il presidente Assad non ha mai tollerato potere parallelo e ha sempre voluto la resistenza palestinese ai suoi ordini. Per il resto dei fedayn, atteso in Iraq, in Tunisia o altrove, il nuovo esilio si-

(Continua a pagina 2 in quarta colonna)

Gerusalemme. Un'immagine dell'incontro fra il ministro della Difesa israeliano Ariel Shar..a (a sinistra), il Primo ministro Menachem Begin e l'inviato americano Philip Habib: il più recente tentativo per giungere all'evacuazione pacifica dei palestinesi da Beirut (Tel. Unite) Press)

Spadolini intanto incontra i sindacati e la Confindustria

Oggi la risposta del psi Lunedì il nuovo governo?

Domani si pronunceranno anche gli altri quattro partiti della maggioranza - I tre problemi più delicati per il presidente incaricato: accordo sui punti concreti della riforma istituzionale, intesa sul programma economico, scelta dei ministri

ROMA — «Il governo si farà in tempi brevi, io ho la più assoluta fiducia in Spadolini: le elezioni sarebbero state un elemento di turbamento per la vita del Paese». Così Sandro Pertini ha raggiunto ieri Beiva di Val Gardena, per una breve vacanza che conferma la spontanea, naturale «regia» gioca-ta dal Quirinale in questa crisi. Lasciando Roma, il Capo dello Stato sdrammatizza infatti questa settimana di trattative tra i partiti, il mette in pratica Spadolini al sicuro da possibili sorprese anche se non tutti gli scogli sono già stati superati per la nascita del nuovo governo.

Restano infatti almeno tre delicati problemi: l'accordo sui punti concreti della riforma istituzionale; l'intesa sul programma economico, la scelta dei nuovi ministri. Ma in un colloquio di più di u...o ra, ieri a Ciampino, Pertini e Spadolini hanno già fissato questo programma di massima: se tra domani e mercoledì di ieri tutti e cinque partiti, il nuovo governo potrebbe giurare al Quirinale all'inizio della prossima settimana, per poi presentarsi per la fiducia alla Camera alla riap....vura del Parlamento, il 3 settembre.

Per ora Spadolini lascia la parola ai partiti, e mentre aspetta che si pronuncino la vora alla bozza di programma economico — che ha parti per

centro l'impegno di contenere nel prossimo anno il tasso di inflazione al 13 per cento; e di curare con sindacati e Confindustria le difficili prospettive dell'aut...o. Intanto ogni giorno la direzione socialista dà rispo... ufficiale dei par al-le proposte del presidente incaricato; e domani si riunirano le direzioni del pdi, del pri, del pli e della dc, per la sanzione formale dell'appoggio al nuovo governo.

Da giovedì, così, se non ci saranno sorprese Spadolini potrà affrontare l'ultimo giro di incontri con i cinque partiti, per discutere gli obiettivi e il programma del governo contro la crisi economica e per la riforma istituzionale.

Spadolini dovrà ancora mediare tra le esigenze dei partiti e il suo programma: e domani a Ciampino. Pertini e ...i contrasti prima della crisi, il riporta questo programma di massima: se tra domani e mercoledì di ieri tutti e cinque partiti, in...dizio della prossima settimana...

L'ultimo ostacolo sarà la lista dei nuovi ministri. Spadolini ha annunciato che vuole avvalersi dell'autonomia che la Costituzione gli attribuisce nella formazione del governo, e si sa che su questa strada Pertini lo appoggia pienamente; ma nello stesso tempo, il presidente del Consiglio ha già detto al Capo dello Sta to che intende «rispettare i partiti» che lo appoggiano, senza far nascere nuovi motivi di contrasto.

La scelta dei ministri sarà dunque un nuovo problema di equilibrio, tra l'esigenza di novità nel metodo e nella forma e le vecchie esigenze del partiti e dei sostegno alla coalizione: entro la fine della settimana Spadolini riceverà ogni partito una «rosa» di nomi per i ministeri; e tra questi nomi sarà poi lui a scegliere i suoi ministri. Per ricevere il presidente del Consiglio una volta. Spadolini scioglierà la riserva e nello stesso tempo presenterà i suoi ministri. Poi, senza riconvocare il Parlamento in anticipo. Si attenderanno i pochi giorni che mancano alla ria...ura della camera per il dibattito sulla fiducia.

Bernardo Valli

Rimarranno i «tagli» alla spesa pubblica

Spadolini prepara il documento economico

ROMA — E' un documento snello, racchiuso in alcuni punti essenziali. Anche per l'economia Spadolini ha deciso di seguire la strada già imboccata per le riforme istituzionali: In questo modo punta a dare ai partiti, chiamati a sostenerlo in Parlamento, un'idea chiara e...precisa di come la muoversi, Nino de Crea, Zanone, De Mita, Longo e Biasini avranno a disposizione il programma per esaminarlo e successivamente discuterlo negli incontri

con le altre forze politiche e il Governatore della Banca d'Italia.

Alcuni passaggi qualifican...del programma economico (sul fronte dell'utamazione sono i seguenti: impulso decisivo alla lotta all'evasione fiscale con la riproporzione del ...riordino degli scaglioni di imposta, sostegno allo sviluppo e ridurre il debito pubblico a...

A PAGINA 11

La Borsa riparte all'improvviso In una seduta guadagna il 3,6 per cento

con il presidente del Consiglio incaricato.

Lo staff degli economisti di Palazzo Chigi ha lavorato anche il giorno di Ferragosto per mettere a punto il documento: che si rifà... la mano dei decreti sulle imprese con una legge finanziaria, ma che tiene conto parzialmente delle osservazioni raccolte in questi giorni dagli esperti nei colloqui con

Eugenio Palmieri

(Continua a pagina 2 in settima colonna)

La se
vuot

(Il Giappone
prende suo
grado un inc.
le grandi pote

DAL NOSTRO CORRISP
TOKYO — U
massiccio momen
co, o un marem
tropicali, con dalle d
oceanico mondiale
stanno nascendo, a
di Occidente, vuole
rompere a nuove frasse
losso. Mentre le tre
nuano, e altre p...
già si intuisce che
dal grande «svippo»
mente disegnando il
mente la prossima
ma del XXI anno...

Celebrata anche a Danzica la nascita del sindacato Solidarnosc

Manifestanti dispersi a Varsavia Jaruzelski da Breznev in Crimea

La polizia ha usato gas lacrimogeni e idranti - Il primate: presto sapremo quando verrà il Papa

VARSAVIA — La polizia ha attaccato e disperso ieri un migliaio di persone radunate in torno ala grande croce di fiori in Piazza della Vittoria a Varsavia per commemorare il secondo anniversario della Stranieri on contratto di sciopero del sindacato Solidarnosc.

Dopo aver intimato alla folla — in quel momento un miglia di persone — di disperdersi, la polizia ha continuato a far uso di idranti. Alcune centinaia di persone si sono inginocchiate in preghiera in prossimiti, della croce e per breve tempo sono state colse dal getto d'acqua.

Di fianco alla croce erano state messe gran i foto d...lori di Lech Walesa e del Papa; era visibile an un e grande striscione con scritto «Solidarnosc». Alcuni artigiani avevano potuto anche un intarsio in legno con la scritta «Wron» (Consiglio militare di salvezza nazionale) che è stato spezzato, in segno di opposizione allo stato di guerra.

Facendo uso anche di gas lacrimogeni la polizia ha completamente sgomberato la piazza. Si è formato tuttavia un piccolo corteo che si è diretto verso la città vecchia Altre persone si sono riunite in alcuni punti al margini della piazza e in prossimità del parroc... la polizia interveniva per sperdere la folla e le manifesta Paechi si trova proprio dinfro il monumento e nella vicinanza. Di fronte al teatro nazionale sono stati gettati vo...anti in favore di Solidarnosc.

Anche a Danzica è stato commemorato il secondo anniversario del comitati interni di sciopero del sindacato. Centinaia di persone si sono riunite in altrosino di fronte al monumento delle 1970; molti migliaia di persone — in quel memomento sono state accolte dai fischi della folla. In serata gruppi di giovani sono stati allontanati dalla polizia.

Ieri il leader polacco Jaruzelski si è incontrato in Crimea con il presidente sovietico Breznev, e ha ottenuto il benestare del capo del Cremlino per la sua politica dopo aver introduzione della legge marziale e la promessa di ulte-

riori aiuti economici per far uscire il Paese dalla crisi.

Il comunicato ufficiale diffuso a Mosca dall'agenzia Tass al termine del colloquio ha però sottolineato che la raffelamente che si ... ralamente nella politica di «progressivo miglioramento della situazione»: In Polonia: si «anno ancora sentire in modo sensibile le conseguenze della crisi econo-

nomica e politica», il cui superamento «viene frenato dall'opposizione al Paese controrivoluzionarie che agiscono nella linea clandestinità e sono ispirate e appoggiate dall'estero, Stati Uniti in primo luogo.

«Può darsi che proprio cominciando dagli agricoltori si sia riusciti a creare il clima di dialogo tanto atteso, tra il governo e la società. Questo dialogo comincerebbe ad affiorare l'intesa e a disarmare l'odio, per l'odio può esistere anche nel silenzio, quando si tiene i denti stretti». A proposito della situazione nel Paese, il primate ha accentuato «la lontana crescente d'unità da parte di uno scontro sul piano delle libertà interiori.

Giemp ha parlato anche del viaggio del Papa in Polonia. preannunciando: «Penso che potrò annunciare ben presto la data della visita di Giovanni Paolo II». Il viaggio del Papa doveva aver luogo inizialmente in agosto; il primate ha detto che «è stato rimandato in attesa che il Paese si riprenda» da tale proposito si attende... il 26 gennaio anche il primate Giemp esprimevo «il mio profondo dispiacere» per il rinvio prolungato della visita del Papa.

Santuario di Chezstochova. Parlando della situazione dei contadini, Giemp ha detto gli appuali dei fedeli.

Scendono i tassi Usa Wall Street euforica

NEW YORK — Per la prima volta dall'ingresso al potere di Reagan un senso d'euforia ha colto la finanza americana. E' l'effetto dell'inatteso calo del tasso di sconto dall'11 al 10,5 per cento deciso dalla Riserva Federale lo scorso venerdì. Essa ha immediatamente prodotto un ribasso del prime rate, l'interesse sta...cio dalle grandi banche per imprese, che 15 al 14,5 per cen...o e in taluni casi al 14 per cento. Sono questi i livelli più bassi degli ultimi due anni, e si prevede che scenderanno ulteriormente. Prima dell'assemblea annuale del Fondo monetario a Toronto il 5 settembre, Riserva Federale dovrebbe infatti ridurre di un ulteriore mezzo punto il tasso di sconto. La misura sarebbe resultata da una nuova riduzione del prime rate.

(Servizio a pagina 10)

SPADOLINI BIS

Ezio Mauro

tato invia... un mi...
lione di anni in al posto delle
altissime montagne dell'Himalaya c'era un altipiano a
un migliaio di metri sul livello
del mare lo dicono i fossili pro-
venienti a 5 mila metri di quota di fossili tipici delle

Ma significa che all'inizio
dell'ultima era glaciale circa
due milioni di anni le colline
tagne dell'Himalaya erano
colline guardate dall'alto in
basso dall'altipiano del Tibet

Vinto il K2
dal versante
della Cina

PECHINO — Per la prima
volta il K2, che con i suoi
8611 metri di altezza è la seconda montagna più alta del
mondo dopo l'Everest, è stato
conquistato dal versante ci-
nese.

Vittorio P.

(Continua a pag
in seconda pag

L'Egitto congela i negoziati sull'autonomia dei palestinesi

IL CAIRO — L'Egitto ha deciso di congelare i negoziati sull'autonomia palestinese che il ritiro totale delle forze israeliane dal Libano: lo ha annunciato il ministro di Stato per gli Affari Esteri. Butros Ghali. Anche il ministro e ministro degli Esteri, Kamal Hassan Ali, ha reso noto di aver informato l'incaricato d'affari americano al Cairo, Henry Brecht, che i negoziati sull'autonomia sulle stesse basi... E' indispensabile fissare un periodo transitorio al termine del quale i palestinesi decideranno del loro avvenire».

I negoziati sull'autonomia palestinese in Cisgiordania e a Gaza, che si trascinano da due anni, sono sospesi dal marzo scorso, avrebbe sospeso le condizioni la se l'Egitto, e riconosciuta dall'Egitto come la capitale dello Stato ebraico.

In viaggio oltre undici milion i di auto e moto

Quasi 800 incidenti, 41 morti il grave bilancio di Ferragosto

ROMA — Quarantun persone sono rimaste uccise in sciagure stradali durante il weekend di Ferragosto E la cifra più drammatica comincia nel bilancio di questi due giorni redatto dal ministero dell'Interno.

Anche a Danzica è stato commemorato il secondo anniversario dei comitati interni ... nestimana, sinao transitati sul territorio italiano oltre milioni 91 mila veicoli. Gli incidenti mortali sono stati trecentodieci — sono poi s...trecentocinque e hanno provocato quaranun quarantun vit... quelli di gravità minore - sono stati 475. Altri il morti sono i feriti 1231 persone.

Interessanti i dati che riguardano la prima metà del mese. Dopronoscente e di prezzo-compreso tra il 29 luglio e il 15 agosto di quest'anno con lo stesso arco di tempo del 1981. Si registra una diminuzione dei veicoli circolanti: 91 milio-

in 934 mila 700 quest'anno. 104 milioni 234 mila nell'81. In leggera diminuzione anche ...il incidenti, benché si siano ri... velati gli orari nell'82: sono aumentate le vittime e sono calati i feriti.

Nel 18 giorni presi in esame — i più cruciali per il traffico nazionale — gli incidenti sono stati dieci...mo e i quasi anno —stati diecimil... i quest'anno (con gli anni precedenti...— stati diecimila 331 del 1981. Nelle sciagure dei periodo estate sono morti un pò cen-totredici e hanno provocato quanti quanti in tutti crescio - sono stati 1983 hanno prov... 7 mila e... 467 mila 475 mi...— dei feriti 1231 persone.

Rincarano gli alimentari all'ingrosso

ROMA — Burro e farina si pagheranno di più nelle prossime settimane: il prezzo ha compreso tra il 29 luglio e il 15 agosto di quest'anno con lo stesso arco di tempo del 1981, si registra una diminuzione dei veicoli circolanti: 91 milio-

latte, costeranno più cari al rientro dalle ferie? Il prezzo al minimo del 2% ad un massimo del 20%.

Secondo l'Anced-Conad (l'associazione nazionale cooperative fra dettaglianti) dalle rilevazioni effettuate al'asso...ne risulta che l'asso...ne risulta che i prezzi all'ingrosso dei prodotti alimentari, con ri...crescerebbero dal leggero rialzo crescito- e. Si tratta di incrementi mediamente «speri.... quelli registrati nel primo semestre 82 che più in atti ed sus... speravano il tetto previsto per l'«flazione.

Questi quesiti inevitabile a settembre, sostengono allo sviluppo - tra i rincari più preannunciati e la differenza il suo aumento ogni anno di u...il quintale di un millimetro. E una differenza che sfugge alla no-

Un millimetro l'anno in più, «premuto» dal subcontinente indiano

Incontentabile, l'Himalaya cres

Si sapeva che oltre un mi...ne di anni fa al posto delle altissime montagne dell'Hi-malaya c'era un altipiano a un migliaio di metri sul livello del mare lo dicono i fossili provenienti a 5 mila metri di quota di fossili tipici delle

stra povera percezione di settimane o migliaia di milioni, e che certo non renders più diff... l'Himalaya... e un altipiano a un migliaio di metri sul livello del mare lo dicono i fossili provenienti a 5 mila metri di quota di fossili tipici delle

l'Himalaya; le m...
sempre più alte han...
caso le correnti calde
che venivano dall'O...
diano, e hanno trasa
in acqua e pieda in
Oggi le cause di que...
lenno sollevamento
malaya sono chiare
continente indiano e
a spostarsi verso Nor...
ma anch'esso e con...

'I normally give away my original drawings to politicians who ask for them. One morning at eight o'clock I received a telephone call from President Pertini [whom Forattini has also portrayed in unflattering poses]. He just said "Forattini, it's Pertini here." You can imagine what happened that first time. I was sure it was a joke, so I said, "Oh, shut up! I am asleep!" and rang off.

'Afterwards he invited me to lunch at the Presidential Palace.'

Forattini gets hundreds of letters each week. 'I believe my satire has enabled the public to laugh more unrestrainedly at their leaders,' he said. 'I get a lot of insults from Communists like "We are a group of Neapolitan workers and we don't like your dirty insinuations . . ."'

'The Catholics on the other hand tend to stand on their high horse and complain about Pope cartoons in pained terms. But you must remember that until only a year or two ago it would have been unthinkable to run a caricature of the Pope in a national newspaper. Now it happens all the time.'

Italy is still very far, however, from stomaching satirical magazines or periodicals of the calibre of *Private Eye* in Britain or *Le Canard Enchainé* in France. And it was not so long ago, the seventies to be precise, that the Vatican Newspaper *L'Osservatore Romano* used to explode with rage every time an Italian publication satirised the Pope. In 1976, for example, the Vatican organ described the re-publication in an Italian weekly of a cartoon that had first appeared in a mass-circulation West German magazine as 'obscene and a grave affront to the Pope'. The cartoon appeared shortly after a Vatican statement on sexual ethics and showed the Pope giving advice on birth control to a married couple in bed.

The following year the Vatican was officially not amused once again. The subject of its ire was a television performance by the Italian comedian Dario Fo, who performed a sketch that had amused audiences all over Europe called 'Funny Mystery'. He took as his target for satire a Pope who died more than six hundred years ago, Boniface VIII. The thirteenth-century Pope had tried, with mixed success, to assert his temporal power, and Dario Fo used the story to mock the whole power structure of the Vatican today, by insinuation.

'Vulgarity,' Dario Fo said, as we talked during the interval of one of his shows in Milan, 'is an essential element of comedy. But everything depends on the context in which it is used.

'One of my favourite sketches deals with the siege of the Papal Legate in Bologna at the time of Dante. The Pope's envoy who had come to negotiate was chased by the crowd and pelted with excrement, and had to take refuge in the castle. In the end, after fifteen days, the Legate gave up and left. It's a true story, but you won't find it in the history books.

'Well, when I told the story in Bologna the audience went into hysterics. They were rolling in the aisles. The context of the story is everything. I explained to the audience why people in those days, just like today, needed obscenity as a weapon against oppression. Machiavelli said that it is necessary to give a sense of shame to the people.'

Dario, who inside Italy is well known for his Communist leanings, and is therefore a predictable target for criticism by the Roman Catholic Church and the Political Right, went on: 'I make people laugh in spite of their politics.

'I went to Spain shortly after Franco's death, and I believe I was the first person to stand up in public and make fun of him once he was dead. The audience was of course predominantly left-wing, but even so it was clear that people were shocked at first. They simply could not conceive that it was not against the law any more to mock the dead dictator after forty years of his rule. The laughs took some time to come. They were strange, strangulated laughs, rather like a horse neighing.

'Better than any other nation in Europe,' Dario went on, 'we Italians know that the Europeans are a brotherhood of peoples, each one of which has had an effect on all the others.

'The British for example like to be provoked in order to laugh. Bernard Shaw understood this. I was performing in England shortly after the Falklands War, and I understood that people were perplexed about events. So I pretended to be perplexed too. I treated the war as a sporting event. They understood that. And then I talked about the soldiers liberating the sheep in the Falklands! They appreciated me making fun of the Italians, and also joking about the Pope. I had to be careful about the Queen, though, jokes about her are not really on, I found. With Mrs Thatcher it was permissible, just.

'In Italy the kind of humour varies enormously from one region to another. In Naples there is a strong Arab flavour to the local jokes. The humour of the Venetians is strongly linked to their particular dialect. The Lombards' humour is conditioned by their long domination by Spain.'

Dario Fo, together with his wife Franca Rame, has taken his special distillation of Italian humour on tour all over the world, an uncommon venture in the Italian theatre which tends to be heavily dependent upon translations of foreign works. In the early eighties Dario took his satirical shows to Britain, the United States, France, Brazil, Japan, Australia and New Zealand. Language, he says, is no barrier for him. He projects subtitles on a screen behind him if he considers it necessary.

Dario has a large, mobile face, but he does not clown to get his audience laughing. His humour is verbal and he frequently retreats into his native dialect of the plains of the river Po.

'Our small fortified towns of northern Italy were and still are a force to be reckoned with,' he told me proudly. 'Remember that the Lombard League, an alliance of only five towns and cities – Milan, Brescia, Bergamo, Cremona, and Bologna – at the end of the twelfth century destroyed the powerful armies of the Holy Roman Emperor who had even occupied Constantinople.

SPADOLINI BIS

1982: Giovânni Spadolini succeeds himself as Italy's Prime Minister at the head of yet another coalition government.

1979: Pope John Paul II learns, one year after his election, that his predecessor, Paul VI, wore a hair shirt 'In odour of sanctity'. Cardinal Casaroli, Vatican Secretary of State, is pulling the laces tight.

'These towns and cities stood for ideals of freedom, independence and justice which still endure. Their town halls were called *Palazzi della Ragione*, meaning, in a double sense, both reason and justice.

'The Romans on the other hand never had any real sense of political or religious freedom, and they display a more cynical type of humour than in Northern Italy.

'I like telling the story of the thirteenth-century chronicler accompanying the Holy Roman Emperor on his way down to Rome from northern Europe.

'They arrive at the gates of Milan, and the chronicler asks someone in the crowd: "Who's that?" and gets the answer: "That's the Emperor with his whore of a wife!"

'The royal party proceeds south and reaches the gates of Rome. The chronicler is there again, and he asks someone in the crowd what all the fuss is about.

' "That's the Empress with her cuckold of a husband!" comes the reply.

'The Milanese, who are easily impressed by titles, regard the Holy Roman Emperor as sacrosanct, while the Romans couldn't care less who visits their city. They have seen it all before.'

Mirella D'Angelo, an up-and-coming young Roman cinema actress anxious to further her career in the legitimate theatre as well, chose a leading part in a satirical play which has been going the rounds of the Rome theatre clubs called *When Popes Had Tails* . . . The play, based on the works of three well-known Roman vernacular poets of the nineteenth and twentieth centuries, Belli, Pascarelli and Trilussa, depends for its comic effect upon a good knowledge of Roman dialect, as well as of the history of the city since 1815. But both she and her audiences appeared to enjoy the experience hugely, at the expense of a lot of anti-Papal and anti-clerical jokes which always go down well in a city where memories of abuses of the Pope's temporal power remain fresh, even though outsiders might consider such events to have been long relegated to the mists of history.

'It was the first time that I ever played for laughs,' Mirella said, 'and I discovered that I have got quite a good sense of humour. I enjoyed the sense of participation with the audience.'

Sabina Manes, co-author of the play, explained to me that she was attempting to convey what that most acute observer of the Italians, Stendhal, noticed about the Romans of his day in the early-nineteenth century, their critical, bitter, disenchanted attitude towards either religious or temporal power.

Stendhal also noted how this sceptical attitude towards power extended to all social classes in Rome.

'Here in Rome,' he wrote, 'music and love are as much themes of conversation for a Duchess as for the wife of her hairdresser – and if the latter is witty there is not much difference. There are differences in fortune, but not in custom. All speak of the same subjects, each according to his or her intelligence. It is one of the elements which strike one about the moral state of this country, the conversation of the greatest nobleman and that of his servant are identical.'

Sabina Manes commented: 'Anyone who lives in Rome knows how this sceptical, resigned humour of the Romans endures. Their humour still deals with carnal love, adultery, and criticism of the government and of the Pope.'

On the whole Italians find it easier to crack jokes and to practise irony in their own local dialect, be it Milanese, Roman, Neapolitan, or Sicilian, rather than in the correct spoken language. There is an audience for foreign funny men; Woody Allen's films in dubbed version enjoy quite a following in Italy, but the humour that is best appreciated always has a strong local tinge to it.

Cinema audiences have dwindled fast with the proliferation of hundreds of local commercial television stations which offer a staple diet of reruns and American soap opera with a heavy accent upon old comedy films. Many Italian towns are now bereft of a local cinema. L'Aquila, for example, a thriving regional capital in the central Apennines which had four cinemas until the late seventies, now has none. Contemporary funny men find it hard to match the success of comic actors of stage and screen such as Eduardo De Filippo, the actor-manager-playwright, and Totò, both Neapolitans, whose local brand of Naples humour has successfully survived on films which show the enormous social changes that have taken place since their heyday in the forties and fifties.

Totò, the dapper, small, mournful-looking film actor who made over one hundred comedies and farces during a long and distinguished career (he was in fact born into a local princely family) is now regarded as the Charles Chaplin of the Italian cinema.

'An unrepeatable phenomenon' was how Alberto Sordi, one of the most experienced comic actors in Italy today, described Totò to me. Albertone, or 'Big Alberto' as he is popularly called, began his career as a comedian on a weekly radio show in the late 1940s in an Italy reduced to rubble by the war and badly in need of something to laugh at. I spoke to him in the cutting room of the film studios in Rome where he was editing his 167th film. He now works more frequently as a director than actor, and has first-hand experience of the varying reactions of audiences all over the peninsula.

'Italy, like Gaul, is divided into three parts, the north, the centre and the south. When I used to play in the theatre, each audience enjoyed itself in a different way. The Piedmontese for example are quite close to the French, colder and harder than southerners, but with a very subtle sense of humour.

'The Milanese,' Alberto continued, 'like to discover things for themselves, you have to be humble in front of them and let them believe they are discovering meanings by themselves. In Rome, they don't laugh at the same jokes as in Milan. And the Romans are much more presumptuous. South of Naples, people react in a much more mortified way, they appreciate popular humour.

'In Tuscany humour is much dryer. In the deep south, people are less open, you have to be careful not to make jokes about the family, about cuckolds. That just makes them indignant. The Mamma is an institution from Rome downwards, you can't laugh at her.'

Alberto's father played the bass tuba in the orchestra at the Rome Opera House. Alberto began his career as a straight actor. 'I didn't have the physique of a comic. Totò, Chaplin and Buster Keaton had something physically funny about them but I just looked like a normal young Roman. I used to be type-cast as a young lover, and complained. Then I met Vittorio De Sica who asked me to make a film with him in 1950 and I was launched.

'I don't play the clown, or try for easy laughs. I began by playing abstract humour. People laugh at me because they recognise in me the truth about themselves. When film directors used to read my scripts they objected that they weren't funny. The comedy is spontaneous, because a husband or wife or mother-in-law recognises the words they themselves use. I owe a lot to neo-realism and De Sica, who took his actors off the street.

'The most serious film I ever made was called *Finché c'è guerra, c'è speranza* [*While there's war, there's hope*]. It is about an arms salesman. Italy is the third or fourth biggest arms-exporting nation in the world today. This salesman goes round third world countries selling weapons of destruction because he has a family making excessive demands upon him. His wife wants jewellery, his sons want motorbikes and to go to nightclubs, they all want a second house, so the poor chap has to go round the world selling machine guns and artillery to kill people.

'Through these images, people laugh. Only afterwards do you realise that the character I played was an abject person, completely immoral. But I made people laugh all the same.

'It's difficult to understand the Italians from outside Italy. Take the economy. Italy has always been a poor country yet its inhabitants live like millionaires. They go on expensive foreign trips and they never bother to look at the bill. Have you ever seen an Italian querying a bill when he's abroad, asking the waiter: "What's this item?" Isn't that the behaviour of a millionaire?

'But you shouldn't judge the Italians from the behaviour of the ones who live abroad. Unlike our French neighbours we have an inferiority complex. The French believe they are superior, more refined, possess the art of living, while the Italian just shuts his mouth when he goes abroad. He's full of complexes because he doesn't know the language, may not have much of an education, and doesn't feel on top of the situation.

'At home here in Italy, however, people haven't got any such complexes. They are living in their own country with such a width of comprehension, such an optimistic outlook that it's quite a contrast with the actual state of politics and the economy.

'No one ever tells Italians how to live, or shows them which path to follow. Each finds his own way to survive. From manual worker to mathematician, he displays qualities of intelligence and imagination and a power of fixing things – *l'arte di arrangiarsi* – which have become a rule of life for survival. I think it's something inborn in the Italian character. I have always tried to reflect the defects in the Italian character in my film roles. The qualities come out through these very defects.

'Italians are diffident, mistrustful. If you tell an Italian to sit down, he'll quickly make sure the seat you offer is not going to collapse. An Italian believes that everyone is an outsider, except his mother, father, brothers and sisters. A wife is an outsider when she first comes into the family.

'These are basic defects. I have been acting for thirty-five years, playing people from every social class, with all these defects, including the ability to survive any traumatic experience, any physical or psychological earthquake.

'Enterprise, cunning, imagination and intelligence – normally these are not at all negative qualities, but here in Italy they are used even when they are unnecessary.

'You English are a trustful people, and if someone offers you his hand, and then tricks you, you react. But the Italian is mistrustful from the start. "Who is he? What does he want?" he asks. He never asks people their name, he couldn't care less. The Italian tells someone he meets on the train: "When you come to Rome, come and look me up." The poor fellow comes to Rome and tries to look him up but of course he doesn't exist, there's no such address. At the moment in question, he appreciates the stranger's company, but when it actually comes to seeing him in Rome, he thinks: "Oh, Madonna, what a bore . . ."

'That's opportunism. Then there's conformity or anti-conformity according to circumstances. Cowardice to save your own skin. You pretend you haven't seen anything. And this leads to *omertà*, the conspiracy of silence.'

Omertà is another Italian key word, usually used in connection with the Sicilian Mafia. It means keeping your mouth shut if you happen to witness a crime, not to involve yourself in any way with officialdom, upon pain of retribution.

'The Italian citizen knows that basically he has no rights, and that protest at the official level will get him nowhere,' Alberto continued. 'It's a relic of Fascism. If an old lady in England trips up over a hole in the pavement, she sues the local authority, the hole should not have been there or should have been signposted, she pays her taxes and enjoys certain rights. Her equivalent in Italy doesn't know whom to sue. She has to act alone. There's no one to back her up. So the Italian develops strong defence mechanisms.'

Alberto appears to have deep convictions about the social importance of his role as a professional funny man. He believes that two of his films actually contributed to important reforms in the law relating to imprisonment without trial, and to the organisation of the National Health Service. Certainly the films in question *Il detenuto in attesa di giudizio (The Accused)* and *Il medico della mutua (The National Health Doctor)* heightened public awareness of problems that still preoccupy many thinking people in Italy.

'Many of my films have shown the audience that in fact there is very little to laugh about. In the opinion of Italian intellectuals, humour is less important than serious drama, because it's rare to find a witty intellectual. As the intellectuals do not know how to make people laugh, they put serious theatre on a pedestal. There are scores of people writing serious drama, but relatively few actually making people laugh.'

Bawdy humour has been appreciated by the Italians since the days of Giovanni Boccaccio, but it is still exceptional to find performers who are capable of exploiting in humorous terms the more open attitudes to sex now prevalent in Italy as in other Catholic countries of the Mediterranean. One reason is a censorship law still based on that which operated during the Fascist period, another is the power of local magistrates to act as self-appointed guardians of public morals if complaints are made about stage or film performances, on the grounds of alleged obscenity.

Franca Rame, Dario Fo's wife and stage partner, has had international success with cabaret-style productions satirising the new sexual mores. Her latest show, however, entitled *An Open Couple – Almost Split in Two* got into trouble in Milan in 1983. This was the flavour of the script:

He: The idea of the closed couple, of the family, is tied to the defence of big business. What you don't understand is that I can have a relationship with another woman and still keep up my friendship with you, have a feeling of love and tenderness, and above all of respect for you.

She: That's a nice phrase! Did you dream it up alone? No more cuckoldry, old Italian style. Now we are to behave like modern, civilised, politically aware people . . . There was this girl, very pretty she was, whom he went out with 'for a joke', he said. She ate ice-cream and was still going to school. He helped her to do her homework.

He: Well, it was like a game. I used to play with that little girl.

She: Yes, they used to play, hiding under the sheets. He used to tell me.

He: She makes me feel like a boy again. And a father at the same time.

She: Yes, a teenage father! Be careful she doesn't get pregnant, I told him. One day he came to me and said . . .

He: Look, these things are better done by women. Why don't you accompany Piera . . .

She: Piera was the name of the girl.

He: . . . to the gynaecologist to get a coil fitted.

She: Yes, of course, take her to the gynaecologist. 'Doctor, I wonder if you would be good enough to fit my husband's fiancée with a coil.' I hope he has a sense of humour like us.
   I'll fit you with a coil . . . in your nose. Crossways, one in each nostril. . . .

The show was banned to minors under the age of eighteen by the Italian Ministry of Tourism and Entertainment because it 'included situations and description concerning sexual relations with explicit language likely to affect the sensitivity of young people.'

Franca Rame wrote to the Minister concerned pointing out that all she was doing was to portray a married couple of the 1980s discussing their problems, problems which were common to many couples of differing social classes. She also stressed that the sketch had been played with great success and no censorship problems in more than eleven foreign countries.

The ban was later rescinded. I saw the sketch play to packed, appreciative houses in Milan, who clearly found Franca Rame's humour to their liking.

For a professional assessment of Italian humour I turned to Franco Ferrarotti, Professor of Sociology at Rome University, a keen observer of contemporary society, to find out what he thought. He was not enthusiastic.

'Italians are portrayed abroad as joyful people with a song on their lips. It's not true. They are rather morose,' he said. 'They have a dark side which is typical of sunny countries. They have a flair for tragedy or melodrama rather than for humour.

'Self-deprecation is only possible when you are secure enough to indulge in self-criticism. Italians tend to be rhetorical. They lack humour about their own physical as well as moral defects. *Commedia all'italiana* is all about appearances. There is not much feeling for tricks of language. Caricatures are rather gross. We do not have any masterpieces of irony in Italian literature.

'Humour implies detachment from the object of your wit. We don't have that kind of attitude. Italians are passionate people who easily identify with what they are talking about. They are too greedy and too eager to be really funny.'

That judgment may apply to the mass of Italians. It does not apply to a professional humorist like Giorgio Forattini, the political cartoonist, who seemed to me to possess the necessary degree of introspection to qualify as a genuine satirist. I asked him what advice he would give to the aspiring political cartoonist in Italy today.

'Stand in front of a mirror, completely naked,' he replied. 'Divest yourself of any faith or ideology and assume the serious and respectable expression of someone who is pretending to be a fervent believer. Then look at yourself and laugh until you can't stand it any more.

'Then, when you are in the crowd and observe the infinite attitudes and innumerable expressions of others, you will realise that you are still in front of that mirror, laughing at yourself.

'It's as if the mirror has broken into a thousand pieces. Self-caricature is the summum of all caricatures. That's why it's never necessary for me to see a politician in the flesh in order to draw him. I satirise politicians without knowing any of my victims personally.

'Of course it also helps if you can draw!'

I suppose the most typical Italian sense of humour remains that expressed in popular dialect sayings still handed on from one generation to the next. This sort of wit is heavily anti-feminist, such as the Calabrian proverb '*A fimmana ndavi i capigli longhi e u sensu curtu*' (Women have long hair and tiny brains), and is distinguished by the close contacts it reveals with traditional peasant life, e.g. the Roman proverb '*La donna è come li cavalli, se conosce da li denti*' (Women are like horses, you know them by their teeth).

For dry wit and wordly wisdom it would be hard however to beat an old, and lengthy, Tuscan saying which seems to sum up a lot of rather bitter experience of life:

'Keep away from sick doctors, rampaging lunatics, sententious men, desperate women, dogs that don't bark, men that don't speak, people who go to mass twice a day, those who play cards for money, deals with thieves, new inns, old whores, night searches, judges' opinions, doctors' doubts, chemists' prescriptions, lawyers' clauses, moneylenders' bargains, wives' tears, merchants' lies, robbers in your home, old enemies, returned servants, the fury of the mob, runaway horses, the scorn of your betters, the company of traitors and gamblers, and quarrels with those who are bigger than you are.'

NINE

The Cows of Father Eligio

> When I was a boy, my father led me by the hand each morning to see the cows in their stalls. He took great pleasure in teaching me how to distinguish an outstanding animal from one that was defective, or just normal: to observe its coat, posterior, udders all straight and equal, its horns, hooves, and a thousand other less obvious but still important details. This rudimentary lesson about cows was to be of enormous help to me during my life in understanding better the world of men.
>
> Father Eligio, Franciscan priest

The accident of geography which caused Saint Peter to be martyred in Rome led to a dominant role, first by Romans, and then by Italians in the whole history of Christendom.

The Calendar of Saints of the Roman Catholic Church carries a quite unfair number of Italian names, and of course for centuries the Papacy remained an Italian fief. In 1978 Karol Wojtyla was the first non-Italian to be elected to the See of Peter in four hundred and fifty years.

Augustine, who converted England, was an Italian. So were Francis, Catherine, Cecilia. . . .

The Vatican has now attempted to correct the balance not only by internationalising the Roman Curia but also by beatifying and canonising the holy dead of other nations and continents. New French, Japanese, Phillipine, Canadian, American, Rumanian and of course Polish Saints and Blesseds are being proclaimed with increasing frequency in Saint Peter's Square, or elsewhere during the Pope's travels.

With the signing of a new Concordat or agreement between the Church and the Italian State in 1984, the Roman Catholic religion ceased to be the state religion of Italy for the first time, I suppose, since the conversion to Christianity of the Roman Emperor Constantine in the fourth century AD.

Yet the Church remains a powerful force in Italian life, not from the diminishing number of people who attend Mass each Sunday, but from the positions of influence that its Bishops still hold in society. The Church is still one of the biggest landowners in Italy, it exercises a profound influence over education (half Italy's non-state schools are religious) and although the Christian Democrats who have monopolised political power in government in Italy since World War Two are no longer a confessional party, they still listen carefully to what the Vatican says.

There is also a strong anti-clerical streak running through Italian life, and it is no coincidence that the huge area in central Italy which used to form the Papal States can be easily identified on modern electoral maps by a solid Communist vote. Memories of poor Papal administration die hard.

In the green hills of Umbria, right in the centre of the former Papal territories, lies the walled mediaeval city of Spoleto. It still has a church around every corner, but is known best today for its annual music and drama festival which attracts visitors from all over the world. Dotted around the surrounding countryside are dozens of monasteries and convents, some in ruins now, but many still occupied by religious, including closed communities whose members never emerge into the outside world.

Nuns are a common sight in Spoleto as they go about their business, shopping for their communities, caring for the sick, the old, and the mentally handicapped, valued social workers in a country where social services organised by the state are seriously lacking.

Sister Genoveffa – Genevieve in English – belongs to a very small religious order called the Sisters of the Holy Family, founded by a local country priest just over a century ago. She was born in Sicily fifty-one years ago, the fourth of a family of six children. She felt her vocation early in life.

'What I remember was this burning desire to be accepted as a nun,' she said, sitting in her study in the large villa just outside Spoleto where she is now novice mistress, in charge of six girls, Marina, Fida, Giovanna, Eleonora, Lucia, and Maria. They too are all hoping to be nuns.

'I made the decision when I was only fifteen. My family was against it at first, above all my father. He couldn't accept the idea that he would not have a daughter any more. But I felt the call within me so clearly and so truly that it would have been a betrayal to reject it. So I set off, and my adventure is not over yet.'

Sister Genoveffa's career has taken her back to Sicily where she worked for six years in an orphanage, to Trevi, a nearby village, where she spent eleven years looking after severely handicapped and mentally retarded women and girls, and to the United States, where she spent three years teaching in a nursery school for the children of Italian migrants.

The period at Trevi was severely taxing. The plight of the handicapped women reduced her to tears for a month when she first arrived, and over the eleven years that she was there she hardly had a proper night's uninterrupted sleep.

Opposite Venice: Although Venetians go by *vaporetto* or water-bus, many tourists prefer to be ferried about by the traditional gondolier

Veneto: Este, near Padua. The wine-barrel market

Ferrara: The lion in winter. The Po delta is a cold place in November
Opposite Pierferruccio Berolo was a professional ballet dancer for over twenty years.
Now he runs a dance school in Venice

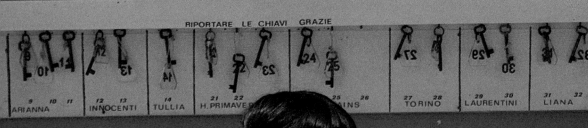

RIPORTARE LE CHIAVI GRAZIE

9 10 11	12 13	14	21 22	23	24 25 26	27 28	29 30	31 32
ARIANNA	INNOCENTI	TULLIA	H. PRIMAVER		AINS	TORINO	LAURENTINI	LIANA

Rimini is now Europe's biggest seaside holiday centre. In the four months of summer those catering for the mass-tourist trade earn enough to live well all the year round. Claudio Casadei *(below)* the *bagnino* has been observing his fellow countrymen at play for over forty years. Rimini was almost totally destroyed in the Second World War but today is one of the most prosperous resorts in Italy boasting miles of hotels along its beaches

Opposite The Casadei family earn £600 a day from renting out beach huts, umbrellas and deck chairs on the sand

Sister Genoveffa Cali from Sicily is novice mistress in charge of six pupils at the Convent of the Holy Family in Spoleto, Umbria

Opposite Umbria: Basilica at Bevagna

The Trevi home for the handicapped, not inappropriately named after 'Saint Mary of the Tears', is a gloomy building inside, despite the beauty of the sixteenth-century exterior; endless dark depressing corridors and sparsely furnished rooms, devoid of comfort. The patients are suffering from paralysis, paranoid schizophrenia, severe physical deformities, mental handicap, or are deaf and dumb.

The medical facilities are good, two doctors attending twice a week plus neurologists and other consultants at regular intervals. There is a music room, gymnasium, a pleasant garden with an aviary, a vegetable and herb garden, swings and see-saws, recreation rooms and a well-equipped kitchen and canteen. The institute is characterless but spotlessly clean. Mother Clorinda and nineteen nuns look after thirty-seven patients. The patients are divided into groups of five or six, and the nuns are on call around the clock.

Mother Clorinda had some hard words against the close relatives of her inmates. 'Most of them simply don't want to know, and never write or telephone,' she said. But the patients themselves are encouraged to talk and think about their families, according to their limited capacities.

Sister Genoveffa got through her period at Trevi with the help of her constant prop – prayer. She now looks back with emotion and joy at having helped handicapped women to recognise her as someone who loved them. 'Spending a year teaching a retarded child to read or write one word was its own reward.'

In 1970 there were over 100,000 people compulsorily detained in state mental hospitals in Italy. Their average length of stay was fifteen years. By 1984, the mental hospital population had dropped by two-thirds as a result of a reform bill passed in 1978. A new radical approach to psychiatry prevents the admission and readmission of psychiatric patients to large public mental hospitals and sets a ceiling on the number of psychiatric in-patient beds ten times lower than in Britain. The new law sees psychiatry in a social, rather than in a purely medical context. However, Italian health and welfare services are administered in a wasteful way, despite the fine intentions of the reformers and legislators, and the health service as a whole is in a disastrous financial position, overspent almost beyond recall. The need for devoted social workers like Sister Genoveffa is greater than ever in a society which is strong in words, but weak in effective action for its chronically sick, its outcasts and drop-outs.

Sister Genoveffa's novices range in age from eighteen to twenty-eight. Once a girl decides she has a vocation she spends a year as a 'postulant'. No vows are taken as she gets first-hand experience of life in a nunnery. The next year she enters the 'novitiate' and wears a simple brown and cream uniform without a veil. She works in the community and takes lessons in theology. At the beginning of her third year she takes vows of poverty, chastity and obedience.

Opposite Sister Genoveffa Cali has been a nun for thirty-five years, eleven of which she spent working at a home for mentally handicapped women near her Order. Behind her is the statue of the founder of the Order – a local priest who died in 1939 at the age of ninety-four

These vows are renewed yearly for five further years, at the end of which she takes her perpetual vows. Few novices drop out of the course, Sister Genoveffa said.

Vocations are falling however. Worldwide the number of nuns in the Roman Catholic Church fell from just over one million in 1974 to about 700,000 ten years later.

Ignazio Maiore is a psychoanalyist who specialises in treating nuns with psychological problems. He believes that there are three types of women who enter nunneries today. 'Some vocations are based on sexophobia,' he said. 'Without realising it, girls try to transfer their sexuality from earth to heaven: in general they are young and good looking, but they become brutally disappointed by the difficulties of life inside a convent, by the vindictive attitudes and frustrations they may find inside.

'Another type of nun is put there by her family. She is generally speaking less intelligent, more pliable, and comes from peasant stock or from the provinces. In any case she is culturally inferior. They are the best candidates. I would call them the professionals of the convents.

'Then there are the nuns from Third World countries for whom entry into a convent is a form of social promotion. But the impact with a different culture can be dangerous for them.'

Sister Genoveffa vigorously disputes this analysis.

'I feel myself completely fulfilled as a woman,' she said. 'I have no frustrations at not having raised a family. I don't feel I have missed anything. I am a normal woman and as such feel the potential of my sex and of my life. I accept them as the gift of God. That is what the vow of chastity means, renewed each day, the promise of a single-minded love of Christ, without any limits.

'Being a woman always means having the desire to be a mother, but it's maternity in a different guise, a spiritual maternity which encompasses pain, sometimes a pain actually greater than that of giving physical birth.

'Our community is not a club, a social group, but a community of faith, hope and love.

'I don't feel I am the teacher of these girls, but their elder sister. When I was a novice myself, I was a disaster because with my character I was always breaking rules, above all the rule of silence. I was incapable of keeping quiet, I didn't even understand its importance. I was a regular chatterbox.'

I travelled back south from Spoleto to Rome, leaving Sister Genoveffa and her charges to their lessons, their prayers, their country walks and mushroom-hunting expeditions, their ordered, structured life which still seemed to leave a lot of time for innocent merriment. Just outside the walls of the Vatican city state, within sight of Saint Peter's dome, I called upon Father Cristoforo, Italian chief assistant to the head of the Franciscan order who at the moment happened to be a Californian.

I asked Father Cristoforo whether the male monastic orders were suffering the same number of defections and the same crisis in vocations as their sisters in Christ.

'We have lost about eight thousand Franciscans worldwide during the past twenty years,' he said. 'We have highs and lows, but today there are some four thousand brothers in Italy and abut thirty-five thousand scattered over the world.

'We are not highly organised intellectuals like the Jesuits,' he went on. 'Nor are we specialists. The followers of Saint Francis are, like him, vagabonds and poets. We don't have "superiors" in our order, we all have enormous freedom, supervised by the group.

'Poverty for us has a value in the sense of liberation. Once you have educated someone to do without money, possessions become meaningless and poverty itself becomes an instrument for action.

'But poverty must not be confused with untidiness, or with bad taste. On the contrary we Italian Franciscans have a sort of collective sensuality about us. If you look at the sites of some of our monasteries you will realise that Franciscans always choose the most aesthetically beautiful places to settle in – it is part of the mentality of the Franciscan family.

'Francis always chose to work among the underprivileged, the rejected, the drop-outs. The leper of today may well be the drug addict. Why don't you go and see for yourself what one of our brothers, Father Eligio, is doing for them?'

I had read in the newspapers about Father Eligio, who achieved a certain notoriety during the 1970s as chaplain to the Milan Football Club, one of Italy's leading soccer clubs, and friend of some exceedingly wealthy, and exceedingly dubious jet-setters.

I finally ran him to ground in an unlikely and distinctly unecclesiastical setting, at Cozzo, a splendidly restored castle dating back more than a thousand years on the edge of Italy's main rice-growing area, fifty miles west of Milan.

Not a blade of grass was out of place in the elegant forecourt. The gravel paths were all carefully raked. In the basement were a well-stocked bar and polished refectory tables. In this sumptuous setting Father Eligio has opened a four-star restaurant (at four-star prices) entirely run and staffed by former drug addicts. It is a huge commercial success, and all the profits go towards the upkeep of this twentieth-century community of rejects of society living according to the spirit of Saint Francis, but drying out without any of the exterior signs of religion, under the iron discipline of Father Eligio. There are no Masses said in the castle of Cozzo, although the former chapel of the Gallarati-Scotti family, who made the property over to Father Eligio in 1974 at a peppercorn rent, has been carefully preserved.

Like hundreds of thousands of other historic buildings in Italy, the castle of Cozzo and its outbuildings had fallen into disrepair as the cost of maintaining such a large estate was too much for the aristocratic owners who withdrew to other properties.

Father Eligio organised a small army of volunteers to dig out the moat, rebuild the stables, restore the unique circular underground ice store, a sort of mediaeval refrigerator, and repoint the mouldering brickwork. He became rather coy when I asked him where all the money for this ambitious and clearly costly restoration project had come from.

'My scandalous friendships with the rich!' he exclaimed. 'Certainly many wealthy people have sought me out. But I was never interested in their money as such, which I see as a tombstone hung around their necks. I have never asked a favour. The rich come to me to ask me favours.'

Father Eligio, in his early fifties, has abandoned the brown peasant habit of his order and the clerical collar in favour of more informal dress, dark blue turtle-neck sweater and slacks. He talks non-stop, and the forty pale-faced former drug addicts who now populate the castle obviously hold him in great affection. He has given them back their self-respect.

'The Lord did not send me to preach to Saints,' he said. 'He sent me to carry out miracles, create scandals, upset people's fat minds. He sent me as a sign of contradiction. Commonplace morals have never been my strong point, rather the terrible path of the Prophet!

'I am not a hermit, nor even a cloistered monk now. However, my fifteen years of cloistered life was my necessary schooling to be with men.'

Father Eligio has opened eleven other drying-out centres for Italy's growing army of drug addicts, in abandoned monasteries and convents in other parts of the peninsula and in Sicily and Sardinia. The only medication he offers is work. A doctor is on hand if necessary but members of these communities accept the thesis of Father Eligio that their cure lies within themselves.

Father Eligio graduated to the drug problem after starting a 'Good Samaritan' telephone service in Milan (two million calls in twenty years), a blood-donor service, and a road safety and courtesy club to try to curb the slaughter on Italy's roads where seventeen million private vehicles now run races. He believes that the established church in Italy is in danger of becoming irrelevant to the real needs of contemporary society. 'How was it,' he asked, 'that the Red Brigades terrorists took as their targets politicians, judges, journalists, managers, but never an Italian priest or bishop? Simply because they are unimportant today.'

The number of deaths in Italy each year as a result of drug abuse has rocketed since 1974 when only eight deaths were recorded. The official figure for 1982 was 252, for 1983 it rose to 360, and the numbers go up yearly. The quantity of hard drugs seized each year by police rose thirty times during the 1970s. The authorities estimate that 1.5 per cent of all young people between the ages of fourteen and thirty are addicted to one or more of the hard drugs and that about a quarter-of-a-million Italians of all social classes and in every part of the peninsula are involved. A 'super-ministry' was set up by the government in March 1984 to co-ordinate the battle against the drug traffickers and there is much closer co-operation than there used to be with the United States' Drug Enforcement Agency, the former Narcotics Bureau. Sicily is a vital link in the refining of heroin imported from Asia for the American drug market, and it was only to be expected that the international traffickers who control the illegal trade should turn their attention to the domestic market in Italy.

Judge Ferdinando Imposimato, who has investigated some of the biggest drug rings operating out of Italy in recent years, believes that the situation is potentially catastrophic.

'There are powerful interests working to destabilise the country, they invest the profits from drugs in sophisticated weapons that end up in the hands of extremist terrorist organisations like the Red Brigades,' the judge told a conference on the subject at Maddaloni, near Naples.

The judge knows what he is talking about. In October 1982 his own brother, who lived in Maddaloni, was assassinated by the Mafia, in an unequivocal warning from the top. An 'oblique vendetta' was how the police described it.

The judge said the traffickers planned to increase the consumption of narcotics by diluting heroin and cocaine they sold and reducing the price in order to attract new users. 'In two or three years time we shall have half-a-million users,' he warned.

The local bishop, Don Antonio Ribera, speaking from the same platform, said despairingly, 'We are no longer in the hands of the Lord, but in the hands of the Mafia and the Camorra.'

In Italy's summer seaside capital, Rimini, the drug problem is worse than anywhere else in the country. There are more arrests for drug offences, more deaths from drug abuse.

Sergio Semprini, a sociologist working in Rimini explained: 'In summer there's a lot of money floating around here, young people get jobs easily as waiters and shop assistants.

'They are not satisfying jobs, but they have one advantage for the young, they are temporary. They work twelve or fourteen hours a day to put together some cash. They keep going on amphetamines, and then when Rimini relapses into its winter desolation they go on to hard drugs.'

The summer crowds leave behind them a human flotsam of drug users who pose serious problems for the local authorities.

Ennio Grassi, a local councillor, said: 'Up till now we never considered the marginal aspects of tourism, but now we are asking ourselves what type of city we really want. And we don't want an Italian Las Vegas.'

Elisabeta Casadei, the Norwegian daughter-in-law of Claudio Casadei, the Rimini *bagnino*, has a sixteen-year-old daughter Cristina.

'Drugs are one thing that really scare me,' she said. 'Rimini is wide open for drug users in summer. And in winter they try to tempt the children outside the schools with sweets and things. I think Cristina is really aware of the problem. When there's a television programme about it I make her stay up and see it.'

Nowhere in Italy is now immune to the drug menace. It has even reached the ancient mountainside villages of Basilicata in the deep south. A young man of twenty died recently from an overdose in the remote and inaccessible village of Guardia Perticara. The nearest centre, Potenza, is fifty miles away along narrow winding roads.

The whole village turned out for the funeral, but the word heroin was never mentioned. The official cause of death was given as 'heart failure'. But this collective silence had nothing to do with the tradition of *omertà*. It was connected rather with the sufferings of countless peasant generations. In Guardia Perticara the old people know all about the land and nothing about drugs. The young know everything about drugs and nothing about the land.

The drug victim had lived alone, without a job, in Guardia Perticara, for eighteen months before he died. He had got into the habit while living at Portici, on the outskirts of Naples. He was not the carrier of the 'white plague' to Guardia Perticara. His peers in the village, boys and girls from seventeen up, had already been smoking pot and injecting themselves with heroin.

In Rome, the use of cocaine is on the increase. A nightclub owner put it like this: 'Cocaine is *in*! Everyone takes it, the idle rich, the sons of papà, adults, young people, criminals, everyone. There are the buyers and there are the sellers. Look at all those cars parked outside. Someone arrives and does his business. My club, within limits, is clean. If I don't like the look of someone, he doesn't get inside. There's always a "heavy" behind the scenes in case of trouble. But you can't watch everyone all the time. And then they take the coke before and after they come here.'

Prince Dado Ruspoli was a jetsetter and playboy of the Rome of the fifties and sixties, the days of the 'dolce vita'.

'We used to have a very good time, but in small groups,' he said. 'Champagne, women, dancing, we were closer to the world of Scott Fitzgerald than to Jack Kerouac. Drugs were a private matter for the very few.

'Unfortunately I was in the thick of it. Morphine, cocaine, heroin. I suffered the torments of hell to escape from the habit and I succeeded, with the help of medical treatment, work, reading, travel.

'I don't think you can talk meaningfully any more about the social classes in Italy, about aristocrats and the middle classes, only about unidentifiable generations and environments.

'I lead a quiet life now with friends. If by chance I go out to a nightclub, I don't recognise anyone. It's like going to the zoo. That's not snobbery, but an objective description of the change.

'We are living in the undergrowth that Pier Paolo Pasolini talked about. The undergrowth without any trees.

'What used to be a phenomenon of the élite, open to criticism if you like, has become a model for mass behaviour with all the consequences that entails. It is difficult for young people to resist drugs because our society has become a sort of permanent propaganda for them. Today we are the slaves of whisky, cigarettes, barbiturates. Perhaps drugs are only just beginning.

'I remember a South American tale. An Aztec king tells the Spanish conquistador: "You want my gold? Take it. We have a leaf that will destroy your world."

'In peasant civilisations drugs have never been a problem. Peasants chew leaves and smoke opium. But when we wanted to transform them and to refine them we created hard drugs, which may prove our undoing.'

According to a 1984 social survey carried out by the church diocese of Rome, the capital has some 50,000 addicts in need of help. It also has 150,000 jobless, 60,000 handicapped, 150,000 old people in need of assistance and 32,000 families sharing accommodation.

Cardinal Ugo Poletti, vicar of Rome and the Pope's chief administrator in his own diocese, realises the social task his Church faces and called upon the Communist-controlled city council to show a more co-operative attitude towards the 3,000 volunteer church social workers whom he said are ready to help alleviate distress. 'Italian society is Catholic,' the Cardinal lamented, 'but at the same time it is anti-clerical.'

What the Roman Catholic Church in Italy has lost in numbers, it may have gained in quality and commitment. Religion as such may have declined, but religious feeling has grown.

Franco Ferrarotti, professor of sociology, put it this way. 'Institutionally speaking,' he said, 'religion has never been taken seriously. Italians have always been Catholics and atheists at the same time. Religion is not an issue in this country. It is the only country in Europe where religion is not a popular issue. Once Pope Pius IX had defined papal infallibility there was no room for discussion any more. Italians are very practical people. If the Pope is infallible, they said to themselves, why waste time in discussion, let's forget about it.'

The dichotomy between Catholicism and Communism that is such a hang-up for Catholics outside Italy troubles few Italians. The late Communist party leader Enrico Berlinguer was quite happy to allow his wife Letizia to practise her religion and attend Mass on Sundays, and to bring up their children in the faith. He once confided to the parish priest of the church where they regularly attended Mass that he felt almost as if he had been there himself, as the sermon was always discussed around the Sunday family lunch table.

Mauro Fiamenghi, the Alfa-Romeo car worker from Turin who is a convinced member of the Italian Communist Party, told me he saw no contradiction between sending his children to church on Sundays and his political beliefs. At one time Mauro gave serious consideration to the idea of becoming a priest.

'The reason I don't go to church now is that I don't have faith,' he said. 'Sometimes I don't go through laziness, and sometimes because at our house up in the mountains I have jobs to do. I find it more convenient to finish off my jobs on Sunday rather than go to church. But I think that my decision about the boys is right until they are seventeen or eighteen and old enough to make up their own minds.

'There's no conflict between Catholicism and Marxism as far as I'm concerned. Having had a Catholic upbringing and having later chosen to be a Communist, I have never experienced this conflict. In fact I find the idea futile and stupid. If none of the Communists in Italy went to church, the churches would be empty.

'Communists know how to distinguish the ideal from the political. No one stops me praying, just as no one stops a Catholic from voting Communist. I believe many Communists don't reveal their faith. They don't want to admit it. But if I go to church I admit it freely. I have no hang-ups.'

On the first Saturday in June 1984, Rome witnessed an unusual event, the wedding in a fashionable church, Saint Gregory on the Celio hill, of Gianni Gennari, a forty-four-year-old former priest and teacher of theology at the Papal University.

Gianni Gennari, for seventeen years a regularly ordained priest of the Roman Catholic Church, fell in love with a schoolteacher from Bologna, Anna Maria Fiengo, and asked the Pope for a suspension from his priestly functions, in order to marry her.

There are nearly six thousand priests in different parts of the world in a similar position, but the Vatican is normally slow to respond, as the present Pope's view is that there can be no change in the status of celibate priests for any reason whatsoever.

However, in the case of Gianni Gennari the Pope gave his personal agreement to a return to lay status. The nuptial mass was concelebrated by no less than ten priests, all close friends of the bridegroom, and there were a score more priests and many nuns in the thousand-strong congregation.

Standing at the altar beside his new wife Gianni said: 'We are here as a symbol, to struggle for a return to the recognition by the church that these two sacraments, marriage and the priesthood, are not incompatible. There should be space in the church both for happily celibate priests and for happily married priests. Unfortunately there have always been unhappy priests.

'Until there is a change of attitude by the church, there will always be problems in understanding the reality of sex and marriage. Women will always be in a condition of inferiority until they enter the ecclesiastical structure with equal rights; I see in the future, as in a dream, not only women priests at the altar, but also couples concelebrating mass.'

Gianni described to me his falling in love as 'a gift'.

The Vatican was clearly not of the same opinion. The publicity surrounding his wedding displeased the Cardinals of the Roman Curia who complained that the dispensation to marry had been granted as a punishment, not as a reward.

Gianni Gennari had been in trouble with his superiors before. He was sacked from one teaching post because he supported the Divorce Law Referendum in 1974. The following year he was censured for writing an article published in the *New York Times* explaining why so many Italian Catholics vote Communist. Then he began writing regularly for Italian newspapers on religious affairs, and since 1979 he has been appearing on a local weekly talk-in show on a Rome commercial TV station, answering viewers' questions on religious or moral problems.

'Most Italians today do not follow the Church's instructions with regard to sexual matters,' he said.

'The watershed was the publication of the Vatican encyclical reiterating the Church's ban on all forms of artificial contraception in 1968. Italians felt reassured by the hostile attitude taken by many of their bishops to the ban and now I would say that they understand that the teaching of the church can be both fallible and reversible. I have had many thousands of letters of support from ordinary Catholics about my marriage who don't really care whether their priests are married or not. The Church's whole attitude to sexuality is negative.'

I asked him whether this was the reason why so few Italian women, in comparison with women in other European countries, take the Pill. (According to figures published by the Population Division of the Rockefeller Foundation in New York, the number of women of fertile age in Italy using the Pill in 1984 was 5.8 per cent. Comparative figures ranged from 38 per cent for Belgium to 28 per cent for France and only 1.9 per cent for Greece.)

'It is a medical problem,' he said. 'It is the fault of the doctors who have exaggerated the risks; and then most Italian men are against it as well. But the true moral problem is not which method of birth control to use, rather the reasons for limiting conception.'

Gianni, like many Italian priests, used to teach religion part-time in secondary schools. One-third of the Italian Roman Catholic clergy are employed by the state as teachers and depend heavily upon these appointments for their living. But under the new Church-State Concordat, religious instruction became an optional subject taken only at the specific request of the pupil or his or her parents.

'I believe that Italians are the most ignorant people in Europe about religion, because it is simply taken for granted here that you know all about it. Children don't go voluntarily to religious classes and the teacher of religion only has credit and credibility if he is a man of culture and has an interesting personality. Within a few years practically no one will be attending religious instruction in Italian State schools, you will see.

'The fact that for the first time in modern history we have a non-Italian Pope means that the Italian church is forced to make its own decisions, and there is great inertia and inefficiency. Italian theologians count for very little. The ones who have the most interesting things to say are all suspect at the Vatican.

'The appointment of many foreign cardinals to the Roman Curia by Pope Paul VI gave the impression that the Church has developed managerial powers, but this is not true. At least the Italian Cardinals, when they were in the majority, used to be conscious of their own limits.'

Although most Italians may not be interested in the niceties of theological debate and are decidedly unimpressed by the Vatican, they are often followers of popular religious practices whose exact origins have long been forgotten. Pilgrimages are well attended, particularly in southern Italy where thousands of believers will follow the annual trail to a popular shrine, just because it has always been done like that. Italian migrants have exported some religious cults from their former villages to American and Canadian metropolises. There is a *Scala Santa*, a replica of the stairs believed to have existed in front of Pontius Pilate's house in Jerusalem, erected by Italian migrants in the Bronx in New York. In a Toronto park, thousands of Italians gather each year to perform Easter rituals and scenes of the Passion which used to be enacted in their villages forty years ago, and which now no longer take place at home as the villages have been completely depopulated by migration.

Inside Italy some ancient rituals persist. Near Benevento for example, in southern Italy, every seven years a mammoth religious procession still takes place to encourage rain in the month of August, for this is a wine-growing area and the rain is needed at this particular moment to enable the grapes to mature properly.

On the Sunday following 15 August, a religious feast day all over Italy, hundreds of people follow a statue of the local Saint brought out into the street. They flagellate themselves until they bleed. They beat their breasts. If a bad drought occurs before seven years are up, the procession is held again, just to ensure that the crops survive.

Professor Lombardi Satriani, an anthropologist from the south who has carried out a detailed study of this ritual, explained: 'If this was a society without technology, you could say that these people knew no better. But in fact they make excellent wine in the Sannio using the most modern techniques. Italians in the south show great cultural invention in matters of survival. Don't forget that the south has always been an agricultural society depending on the success of its crops and at the mercy of uncontrollable events such as drought, floods or earthquakes.

'Southern peasant culture is centred around death,' Professor Satriani continued. 'The experience of dying, the fear of not being able to react properly to such an event, the death of a loved one, has meant the creation of a complex strategy to enable people to face and conquer death.

'It encompasses hundreds of rituals, beliefs and customs which originated with the aim of re-establishing contact between the living and the dead. It's a society which has expended a lot of effort on creating this metaphysical dimension. It's not a cult of the dead. There's nothing necrophilic about it. It is an attempt to reaffirm the values of life.'

In 1984, a parish priest in one Calabrian village, Soveria Simeri, who prided himself upon his 'modern' outlook, thought he would discourage the long local funeral processions by levying a special fee per kilometre upon the family of the deceased. His bishop promptly transferred him to another part of Italy. Attempts by the civil authorities in two other Calabrian towns to ban funeral processions from main roads failed after a local referendum showed popular feeling was against the ban.

'In the south, the family includes the living *and* the dead,' Professor Satriani explained. 'There are reciprocal rights and duties. The dead have to protect the living, and the living have to keep alive the memory of the dead.

'This is the explanation of the *faida* or vendetta. An offence against the honour of the family is handed on to the next generation.

'In the south, relations are between families rather than between individuals. There is also a strong dimension of family sacrifice at the expense of the individual values prized in the rest of the European industrial society.'

The continuities of life through the generations are felt deeply by Italians from all parts of the peninsula. Ferruccio Berolo was born at Belluno in the foothills of the Alps and often returns to the church where he was baptised.

'I was brought up as a Catholic like everyone else in my generation, but I don't go to Mass very often. The church, and religion, for me is the moment when I feel I must sit down and rest, not just my body, but my soul.

'I am particularly fond of the church in Belluno where all my family was baptised and married, and where they started their journey towards eternity. Apart from the beauty of that church, it gives you the sense that life is rather like standing on a bridge. If you look in one direction, you just see life going past, and that's a bit sad. But if you turn your head the other way, you see the water all alive rushing towards you.

'Going into that church I understand that life really has such a marvellous continuity, that this is the place where my life started, and that of my ancestors, and where their lives stopped and where, probably, I hope, my own life will stop. That gives you a sense of peace and quiet. Everything seems to settle down into its proper place. You feel you belong to a much bigger dimension, and that feeling gives me an immense sense of peace.'

In the garden of his villa on the slopes above Prato in Tuscany, filled with cypress trees, oleanders, and pieces of his own terracotta sculpture, Leonetto Tintori has been building his own tomb, and that of his wife Elena. It is in the form of a giant Noah's Ark, as large as a sizeable private yacht. On the outside the figure of Noah peers anxiously out to see if he can spot dry land. The animals are also gathered at the bars of the windows trying to see out, and some of them have muzzles and paws protruding. It is a witty treatment of a theme which Leonetto has seen painted on the walls of countless churches he has restored.

You have to bend low to get inside his Ark, but when you raise your head there is a surprise. A long, low chamber is decorated, like the outside of the Ark, with coloured terracotta panels. At the end are two lifesize statues, one of Leonetto and one of Elena, being consumed by purifying flames. On one wall there is a bas-relief of a trestle table with a white cloth laid for supper with eggs and bread, and twelve stools.

On the floor, two sets of footprints lead towards the statues and a small tabernacle at the end.

'There are two pathways,' Leonetto explained, 'one is Elena's with her actual footprints, and the other is mine, with my own footprints in the clay. The footprints meet, as they do in life, and after walking together we each go into our own place, beyond life.

'There are urns for our ashes with our original signatures, and underneath, just to be on the safe side, we have put our tax code numbers. That is in order to be in perfect accordance with earthly laws.'

Pointing to the statue of Elena on the right, clutching a bunch of flowers, for she is a keen gardener as well as a painter of floral scenes, Leonetto said: 'That's Elena with her flowers, and there I am. I see myself as something empty, shrunken, insubstantial.'

His own statue is indeed partly hollow.

'In the other life,' Leonetto went on, 'we leave our empty shells behind, and in my opinion the best of us returns to the whole, the spiritual whole from which it may go on again into the lives of other people.

'I have almost felt within me tiny particles of Giotto and Filippino Lippi, of Michelangelo and other artists. Their spirit, enclosed in their works, has come down to me.

'I don't know if it is because of his happiness in living for his painting, but I have alway felt very close to Filippino and to his father Filippo. As for Giotto, he is the greatest of all, but I have always been a bit in awe of him. In my opinion Giotto is greater than Michelangelo because he had a simplicity which can never be surpassed.'

It took Leonetto about ten years between the time he conceived the idea of his Ark-tomb and its completion. His wife Elena was not enthusiastic at first but she changed her mind later.

'The Ark has two levels of symbols,' Leonetto went on. 'One is the exterior, which represents the Ark when it came to rest on dry land after the Flood. It represents the sense of liberation from the nightmare of war and from the most tragic things that can happen to one in life.

'Inside, the symbols are more personal. It becomes a refuge for our future life. Elena feels quite calm about it, she feels quite happy to come to her rest inside here.

'We built it with our own hands. Everything came not just from our minds, but from our own physical effort as well.

'We have tried to put in it all the symbols in which we believe. Faith in Christ is present here with the table. The stools are waiting for the Apostles who are coming to this Last Supper, and we hope that in spirit we also shall take part in this meeting.'

Leonetto's Ark is already part of the Tuscan landscape.

TEN

Face to Face

> *Va in piazza e pija consijo; aritorna a casa e fa come te pare.*
> Go into the square and ask for advice; and then go home and please
> yourself.
>
> Roman saying

In December 1970, shortly after Italians became legally entitled to divorce their spouses in a civil court of law for the first time since Napoleon left their country over a hundred and fifty years before, a young social worker travelled to a remote village in the highlands of Calabria to carry out a survey.

She polled the male population to try to find out what would be the reactions of husbands if they discovered their wife in bed with another man.

Over half the husbands replied without hesitation: 'shoot her', and the rest were torn between throwing her out into the street and calling the police. None suggested divorce as a possible solution.

A similar question to wives concerning the possible infidelity of their spouses elicited the practically unanimous answer: 'Keep my mouth shut.'

Traditional attitudes to relationships between the sexes, to marriage, and the family die hard, despite the very considerable social revolution which has taken place in Italy since World War Two. The Divorce Law did not open the floodgates of promiscuity as some more reactionary churchmen such as Cardinal Siri had forecast; there were about one-tenth as many divorces granted in Italy in 1984 as in Britain. After an initial rush to the courts in the early seventies by long-estranged couples anxious to sort out their legal position, the number of applications settled down in the early eighties to a steady thirteen thousand a year. The number of legal separations has gone up, but this reflects more attention to family legal and financial considerations than a desire for change in matrimonial status *per se*.

Marriage as an institution is certainly becoming less popular. There was a twenty-six per cent fall in the number of marriages celebrated during the decade between 1972 and 1982, and an even larger percentage drop in the birthrate. More couples than ever before are choosing to marry at the Town Hall rather than in church, although about eighty-five per cent still prefer a traditional church wedding with all the trimmings. Italian women have suffered a drop in fertility which puts them on a level with women in countries such as Denmark

Legal Separations and Divorces (Divorce Law passed 1970)

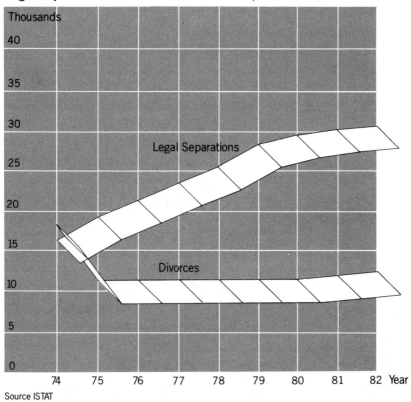

Thousands

Legal Separations

Divorces

74   75   76   77   78   79   80   81   82   Year

Source ISTAT

Births and Legal Abortions (Abortion Law passed 1978)

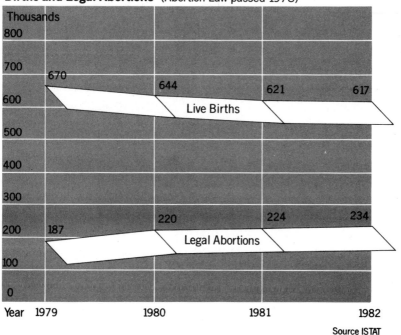

Thousands

670

644

621

617

Live Births

500

220

224

234

187

Legal Abortions

Year   1979   1980   1981   1982

Source ISTAT

Birthrate

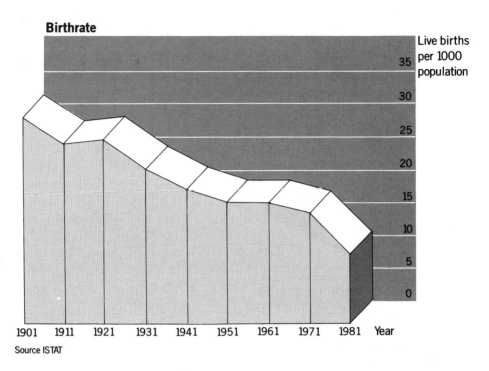

Live births per 1000 population

Source ISTAT

and the Netherlands, normally associated with much more sophisticated social attitudes.

The Italian male is no longer, by law, the uncrowned king of his family. Until the new Family Law of 1975 came into force he could beat his wife with impunity, had undisputed control of the family finances, and the last word in the education of the children. Now all that has changed, in theory. Husbands and wives are equal before the law, own their property in common and have to decide together how their children are to be educated.

In the highlands of Calabria, following the trail of that surprised pollster on divorce in the seventies, I went to talk to a bride of 1984 just before her wedding. Twenty-year-old Fortunata (Natina) Manglaviti, confirmed to me that attitudes to the family in the small villages of southern Italy are evolving very slowly indeed; during her year-long engagement she had never been able to be alone with her fiancé Natale, from the nearby town of Reggio Calabria.

'There's not much chance of amorous adventures in this village,' Natina said. 'Everybody knows everybody else and I didn't find the village boys very special. We are full of taboos here.

'As my father would never allow an affair, the only way out was an official engagement. My parents respected my choice.

'During the engagement we have never been out together alone to a cinema or to the beach, always in the company of a sister or brother-in-law. Here they have that sort of mentality. They begin to whisper and gossip. I personally couldn't care less, but my father would get very angry, I imagine.

'It's very difficult here to get to know your fiancé well before you marry. You can literally never be alone together. Here, the bridegroom is allowed to do what he likes, but the bride has to remain chaste and pure. If she were to go with her fiancé, this purity might not exist any longer.

'When you leave school, there's almost an obligation to get married. But I suppose if you don't find the ideal man you can wait. There's no entertainment or possibility of work in the village. Staying in the house all day you feel the need to get away, have your own home and children.

'I am not very modern,' Natina conceded. 'I'm uneasy about it sometimes, but it's difficult to get rid of certain taboos. I hope however that I shan't pass these taboos on to my children.'

Feudal times lie in the very recent past in Calabria. The *jus primae noctis*, the right of the local baron to enjoy the favours of any peasant bride before her wedding, was only abandoned within the living memory of some elderly villagers in the rugged Aspromonte. And in one village, they are still talking about the extraordinary events of 1983 when a local girl, after a five year engagement to a man she did not love, defied her parents and broke off the match. Her father pointed a pistol at her head and threatened to kill her unless she married her betrothed. She told her father to go ahead, but his courage failed him. The girl is doomed to spinsterhood unless she moves away. She is now twenty-two- years-old, and still living in the village of Cardeto.

Giuseppe Manglaviti, Natina's father, took a more enlightened view.

'Here, when your children reach a certain age, the father has to arrange their future,' Giuseppe told me. 'My daughter had a free choice. But the father has to warn his daughter, this man is all right, or he is no good, he's a criminal; however, he normally gives his consent. The wedding is going to cost me about £25,000 by the time we have paid for the dowry, the furniture, the linen, the hire of the reception hall, the party for six hundred guests; you have to save up for many years; but it is of fundamental importance for us to fix up our eldest daughter, to see her launched.'

The unmarried woman has no status in Calabrian society, so it is essential to get her 'fixed up' as soon as possible. One Calabrian dialect saying compares the spinster to bread without yeast. Another runs: 'daughter in the cradle, trousseau in the drawer' – a warning to prudent mothers not to delay in collecting a trousseau and a dowry for their baby daughters. And a third rhyming proverb reflects the violence which frequently awaits those who transgress social codes in primitive societies:

A fimmana, quandu riva a quindici anni,
O a mariti, o a scanni!

(When a girl gets to fifteen, either you marry her off, or you slit her throat!)

City girls in most parts of Italy might appear to be living on another planet from Natina, to judge by the freedoms they customarily enjoy in the eighties. Claudio Casadei, the *bagnino* in Rimini, who has been a keen observer of the sexual mores of Italians on and off the beach for the past fifty years, put it this way.

'Once you had to court a girl, now if you are not careful she courts you! It is no longer as simple as it was; in our day you had to be someone to conquer a girl. Now it's too easy, love isn't beautiful any more, that's my opinion.

'Have you ever seen little pigeons cooing? That was love. Love is a very delicate thing. Now, it's not considered so important, couples meet, they kiss, and boom boom boom. Then they go somewhere and dance. But call that dancing? They move and they shake, but that's not dancing. Dancing for me means having a girl in your arms. Nowadays, I dance with you, I dance with him, I dance with her, you don't know with whom you are dancing any more.'

Surprisingly, perhaps, discos don't hold much appeal either for Mirella D'Angelo, who was born and brought up in Rome, almost five hundred miles north of Natina's Calabrian village. Mirella at twenty-eight is dedicating her life for the present to film acting. She never suffered the constraints of village life, and as a city girl was able to pursue the career of her choice. She lives alone with a Persian cat called Gemma. She was married once, but the marriage didn't work. Now she puts her career before her personal life.

Mirella is perfectly aware that the facts of life in the Italian cinema and television industry make it extremely hard for her to become a star in her own country on her own terms. She knows that the most successful Italian actresses, such as Anna Magnani and Sophia Loren, gained wider fame outside Italy, and feels she may well be forced to turn abroad in order to advance further in films.

'Italy is the country where there's least space of all for a film actress,' Mirella admitted. 'The only films which are a commercial success here are stupid comedies or films where women are sex-objects.'

When Mirella made her first film in the seventies, Italians were going to the cinema five times as often as people in Britain, where television had taken a firm hold over mass entertainment. Since then, proliferating commercial television has stolen cinema audiences in Italy too. The Italian commercial cinema is dying on its feet with only about thirty films planned for 1985, a tenth of the number of productions completed annually a decade before. Even producers like Federico Fellini find raising money for new films more and more difficult.

Mirella's face was noticed in a Rome street by a perceptive make-up artist when she was only seventeen. He asked her to model a new line in eye-kohl. Within a year she had rocketed to the rank of a highly-paid international fashion model, working in Paris, New York, and London, as well as Rome. But she found the job basically boring, and was tempted by a film part in Paris while still carrying on working as a model. Later she financed a seven month spell at a New

York actors' studio with the pay she received for just one photo-modelling session a week.

In ten years, Mirella has succeeded in landing an average of only one film part a year, including a lead opposite Jean-Paul Belmondo in one French drama, the part of a Roman girl raped on her wedding day by Malcolm McDowell in the American soft-porn epic *Caligula*, and several films aimed mainly at Italian audiences. She has now given up fashion modelling altogether, and has turned to fringe theatre to keep acting while the Italian film industry is in the doldrums.

'My agent thinks I am an idealist and a dreamer,' Mirella said. 'Perhaps in one way I am, you know. He would like me to be a stupid actress. I may not earn very much money now, but at least I am free.

'If I had a protector, I think I would become famous very quickly. Many people let me understand that if I were to become their mistress they could help my career. Some girls go like crazy with these people, but they never arrive, you know.'

Although Mirella played the part of a professional night club stripper in one French film, the experience clearly was not a pleasurable one and she resolutely refuses to pose for nude pin-up photographs.

'Eroticism for me is not taking off my clothes,' Mirella said. 'If a director said to me, "Mirella, I want you to take your clothes off," I should just tell him "Fuck off."

'One director did tell me that if I became his girlfriend I would become a famous actress and I had a long argument with him. It was disgusting.

'There are more possibilities in television now than there used to be, but this involves another problem. Italian television is controlled by the political parties and you need a political as well as an artistic protector in order to get on.

'In the end it is more amusing – and satisfying – to advance through one's own talent. I know people in the film business who like me and esteem me and have confidence in my talent. That is what is important to me.'

Mirella's former husband was a production manager in films. 'My marriage lasted eighteen months,' Mirella said, 'but we started to argue after just one week. I suffered, because even if I think I am not a typical Italian, marriage is always something that counts.

'My former husband was very jealous of my career. Freedom in love is the most important thing for me. Freedom means to love somebody and to accept the other person as he is. I think jealousy is natural, but you have to keep it under control, and be creative with the other person.

'I think Italian men don't really love women, don't really like them. Although my husband was Italian, I get on best with men from outside Italy.

'There's a Mirella in me who is very sociable, sweet and nice with people. And there is another one, very determined and clear in her own mind about what she can and what she cannot do.'

The number of Italians living alone by choice, like Mirella, shot up to about six per cent of the total population during the 1970s, but the family, the blood-related group that meets together regularly each day and shares food, shelter and resources, still remains a powerful force in Italian life. What Italians look for in the family is the continuity and the security that they do not find in the world outside. It gives a focus to their existence.

'The key to the Italian character,' Franco Ferrarotti explained to me, 'is family orientation. I am not speaking of the family only in the conventional or formal sense, but of the family as the privileged place for primary face-to-face relationships. What defines the Italian character, if such a thing exists, is the predominance of direct, face-to-face relations over and against formal official relationships.

'It all has to do with the fact that Italians have had a difficult history. The institutions have changed, rulers have come and gone, people have to survive. And people do survive, thanks to their personal, unofficial relationships. So a primary, first-hand knowledge of any person or problem is absolutely top priority.

'At the same time, there is a proportional distrust of anything that is official. In any other country if you say that a thing is official, it is just that. But here in Italy if you say it's official it means it's probably not true.

'If you have a social life based on primary relations and not on legally established norms, then you must practise the exercise of unpredictability. You learn through experience, not by following the book. Any primary relation, unwritten, always confronts you with the unexpected. It's always dramatic and always ambiguous. You never know how it is going to end. It's not written down anywhere. There is no test. You have to play it all the time as if it's the first time. That's what makes Italian life very difficult and at the same time very charming.

'This applies to the most simple things. Italian problems are not real problems, they are usually problems of bad administration. Every time you have to cash a cheque at the bank, get a permit or a driving licence, it is a real trauma. You learn that in social life all people are not equal. You have your enemies on one side and your friends on the other. So you get to learn a lot about life. If you stick to the rules too closely you are likely to be considered stupid. That's why you can adapt easily in Italy. Because Italians have always adapted. It's like teaching a fish how to swim.

'The good point about not relying on the written norm is that people learn to adapt through experience and personal knowledge. The negative side is that it easily turns into political patronage and also into Mafia crime, because the corruption of primary relations means criminal solidarity.

'If we could only ally this flair for personal relations with modern flexible legislation, and good public administration, that would be marvellous. The drawback of Italy is the attitude of the petty bureaucrat who does everything for his family and friends and nothing for the rest of society and who considers the impersonal citizen as a nuisance.

'The family spirit colours everything,' Franco Ferrarotti continued. 'It is a shock absorber. The laws permitting divorce and abortion have had no real effect. The family means you cannot touch basic values through the law.

'The reliance on face-to-face relations is the reason why Italians are good businessmen. They can sell anything to anyone, provided you agree to talk to them, in the first place.

'It's a human quality that's not exportable. It has to do with this tremendous friction, this exchange of sensations, this culture of touching. You see things through your fingers. When Italians meet they keep on touching. It's not just the feeling of girls' bottoms on buses, but something that comes from far away.

'There's been a decline in Machismo in Italy. Sex is coming to be seen more and more like exploration. There is a value of tenderness creeping in. This fits in beautifully with the Italian mode of doing things, with this idea of knowing through touching, without really conquering anything. I would say that by and large young people have rediscovered love as a way of knowing and tenderness.

'Stendhal understood the Italians. He put it all in a nutshell. If you have a problem, if your lover betrays you, in Paris you have a verbal dispute. In Italy you have a stroke of the stiletto. The French talk, while the Italians act. But it's not like Stendhal thought, that we are more passionate. Once again it's this touching, this primal person-to-person relation that cannot allow any kind of dispute according to a formal code of behaviour.

'Italy is a no man's land poised between rural and industrial society. What we have here is a peculiar sort of Mediterranean industrialisation, in which the impersonality of large-scale organisation is mitigated by the human touch.

'There's always this love affair with the aesthetic side of a problem. What seems to be typically Italian is this attitude towards the machine, in which the idea of taste is dominant. The machine is there, just like any other place in the world, but you also have design and taste as well.

'What seems to me to be typical of Italy is that you have residual attitudes which endure and adapt. An example is the way you hire people. You have no hire and fire policy like you have in the United States or in Britain. You go through personal connections and recommendations and that's what I call the mitigating factor.

'I think in the end we shall come up with a different model of industrial society. We will create something new in which there will be two basic traits: first an aesthetic vocation, and second a great emphasis upon personal relationships.'

I would add a third trait: attachment to place. It was expressed by the hero of Alessandro Manzoni's classic nineteenth-century novel *I Promessi Sposi (The Betrothed)* when he left the familiar shores of Lake Como to seek his fortune.

Farewell, mountains rising up from the water, reaching up to the sky; jagged peaks, known to him who grew up in your presence, and impressed on his mind no less than the faces of his own family; torrents whose individual murmur he recognises, just like the noises in his own home. Dreams of riches lose their attraction at this moment. He wonders how he ever managed to make the decision to leave and would turn back if he did not believe that one day he would return . . .

In the disordered cities, with houses on top of one another and streets that lead only into more streets, he can hardly breathe. Standing in front of the buildings admired by foreigners, he thinks back uneasily to the church tower in his village, to the little house he cast eyes on a long time ago, which he'll buy when he returns to his mountains, a rich man.

The micro-reality of the familiar world of childhood and family is something that Italians cherish the more strongly, given that so many of them have been forced to abandon it for economic reasons. Places tend to become endowed with almost magical qualities.

A journalist writing in 1984 in one of Italy's leading serious newspapers about the Parmesan cheese industry in Parma was able to write as follows without so much as a smile:

The mystery is this: why is it that genuine Parmesan cheese matures naturally only on the banks of the river Enza, near Parma, and imitations from all over the rest of northern Italy can only be ripened artificially with chemicals and formaldehyde which gives it a vague smell of the mortuary? Perhaps it's something in the air, the air that makes the best sausages mature at Zibello, the best violins in Cremona, and the best hams in Langhirano.

Italians remain terribly sensitive to local dialect, in spite of the spread of the standard language all over the country during the past century. Romano Prodi, at the head of Italy's State Industries, was born in the wealthy province of Reggio Emilia, and he still prefers to live in Bologna, although he has to commute 250 miles by air to Rome to work.

'The fact that I was born in Reggio Emilia is basic,' he said. 'We still do not all speak the same language in Italy. I cannot understand a lot of words in the Bologna dialect, and that is only fifty miles away from where I was born.

'The history of foreign occupation is written into our dialects. For example the lira, our currency, is called in dialect the 'franc' in one village near my home town and two miles down the road it is called the 'pfennig'. While I was at school in Bologna, I could detect what part of the town someone came from, north, south, east or west, just by listening to his accent.'

Ferruccio Berolo, an articulate and enthusiastic Venetian by adoption, for he was born in the foothills of the Alps at nearby Belluno, explained how he is sometimes torn between his allegiances to place.

'I saw Venice for the first time when I was already an adult. I stepped on to a bridge, and knew instinctively I had arrived home. Venice for me is the city of the soul. Sometimes I feel split in two because my original roots belong up there in the mountains in Belluno where I was born. But I also belong to Venice now. Sometimes I feel like a seagull that floats between water and air, but belongs completely to neither element.

'I adore Venice in winter when it has got that softness that only winter light can give. It's as if the city were covered with a golden veil, and the shadows are dark and golden as well. When you are in love with a person, you don't worry about the details – I feel the same way about my city. Different details every day. One day, the bricks, all the different shades, from palest gold to dramatic red. Then the stones, and the day after, the light on the canals. And then the next day perhaps I don't like it at all because I am in a bad mood; you know how it is when you get up in the morning and you can't bear the sight of your partner. Being in love with a town or a person is discovering each day something new, and fortunately for me, I am in love with my wife, and in love with my town.

'It's the little discoveries that make love alive and interesting, not something that is framed and written in large letters.

'I know that Venice can be noisy. Italians are known everywhere as noisy people, but at least the noise is human voices, not motor cars.

'It is a civilised place. It's a town built for human beings. You will find people in a hurry here like anywhere else. What do you have to do? Walk a bit faster. You don't have to jump into those horrid things called motor cars and storm all over the place poisoning thousands of people with the exhaust fumes and deafening them with your horn. No, no, no, Venice is a place where man can live in a human dimension.'

My distillation is almost complete. I have let my chosen representatives express the ideas and feelings they have about themselves, their compatriots, and their country at this particular moment in their long history. I have conducted the reader on a whistle-stop tour through a landscape that is uncharted, simply because Italians are normally too busy adapting to rapid change to stand back and observe themselves, while foreigners rarely enjoy the privileged viewing-post of the professional foreign correspondent, with his wide social and linguistic access.

I can already hear the chorus of criticism by sports fans who are incensed by my failure to deal adequately with Italians' passion for soccer; by students of

Italy disappointed at my sketchy account of politics; by those who know other Claudios and Francos and Giovannas and Giuseppes and Mirellas and Albertos and Angelas whom they feel would have been more representative (whatever that may mean in an Italian context).

I make no apologies for bias. My only hope is that this social panorama may help to dispel some of the more foolish stereotype ideas about Italians that circulate in other countries, even if some prejudices are confirmed by my account.

What may be less obvious is that many Italians who left their country to make new lives overseas are equally ill-informed about the social and consumer revolution that has been taking place in their native land.

The scars left by centuries of migration are still in course of healing. Sometimes the wounds of depopulation are still apparent, as in the town of Montemilone and hundreds of other similar southern communities drained of their young men, who were forced to the cities of the north, or abroad, to find work and survive.

Much of the migration was illegal. The most widely-used derogatory word in English-speaking countries to describe Italians has as its origin the wave of illegal migrants to the United States in the 1920s. They were catalogued by their host country, which turned a blind eye to the influx, as WOPs (without official papers) and the term stuck. An Italian became synonymous with a worker of low educational attainment willing to be employed for long hours at low wages because of his unofficial status.

'Little Italies' grew up in metropolises all over North America, with their own churches, shops and cafés, and it was to these ghettoes that the next wave of legal migrants was attracted after World War Two. These communities were in the tradition of the North American garrison; the early settlers raised wooden stockades to protect themselves from the surrounding Indians. The Italian immigrants threw up mental barricades to insulate themselves from the surrounding alien Anglo-Saxon culture. They carried on village life three thousand miles away from their native villages as if nothing had changed, visiting relations on Sundays, playing cards at the bar or *bocci* (a kind of bowls) in the park, and attending social clubs named after Marconi, Leonardo da Vinci or Garibaldi.

At home, Mamma still cooked the *minestra*, although the children were acquiring a taste for hamburgers and Cokes. But the grandparents still spoke to their grandchildren in local village dialect.

The 'Little Italies' of Canada produced second and third generations of English- or French-speaking Canadians uncertain of their cultural identity. A few, caught between cultures, returned home for visits which sparked off new experiments in literature, born out of a deeper understanding of the predicaments of their own families as they were growing up.

One Italo-Canadian writer, Marco Micone, wrote a play, published in 1982, called *Les Gens du Silence*, which takes as its theme the problems faced by Italians who settled in Quebec and had to choose between the use of three languages, English, French, or their native Italian. They had, however, a fourth choice, the language of silence, which gave the play its title.

The Italian government has never been over-solicitous about its scattered tribes. When the migrant liners left Naples for America during the peak years of transatlantic migration, the King of Italy ordered a military band to give them a musical send-off on the quayside. It was not a gesture that was particularly appreciated by the steerage-class passengers.

Years later, when a disastrous earthquake struck near Naples, while government relief columns were still being mobilised or had not yet arrived, survivors with relatives in such distant countries as Venezuela or Australia were not at all surprised to see their kinfolk arrive by air in a matter of hours in their stricken villages all the way from Caracas or Sydney to help. Many decided there and then to leave Italy for good, to join their families established overseas, without waiting for official relief. Within a week of the earthquake, which took almost three thousand lives, ten thousand more Italians had left their native land for ever. They had passed a vote of no-confidence with their feet.

Overseas the Italians do not enjoy the reputation of being valorous fighting-men. In the market in Addis Ababa in Ethiopia, an Italian ex-colony, I once bought a naif painting of Italian soldiers being put to rout by Ethiopians and stopping up their ears to drown the sounds of battle. In Libya, another former bit of twentieth-century Italian empire, they still show Italian soldiers being cut to pieces in battle on the postage stamps. And for how many people in Britain of a certain age is one stereotype image of an Italian that of a prisoner-of-war?

Yet modern Italy's military record is by no means devoid of feats of bravery and sacrifice; Italian armies have had their moments of glory, as well as of defeat, since the days of Garibaldi and his Thousand. Military supremacy is simply perceived today by ordinary Italians as a costly illusion. It took considerable pressure from the United States for Italian troops to be committed to a war-zone for the first time since World War Two when it was decided to send Italian soldiers to Lebanon as part of the multinational peacekeeping force in 1982. But it came as no surprise to most people in Italy to learn that when the expeditionary force set out eastwards for Beirut across the Mediterranean, their transports broke down for lack of maintenance and took an unconscionably long time to reach their destination.

More than eight thousand Italian soldiers, marines and navy men saw service in Lebanon and earned themselves a reputation for diplomacy in a tense and dangerous situation, and for humanitarian work. They set up a field hospital where they treated sixty thousand people of all nationalities and religions, and being fellow Mediterraneans, they enjoyed a relationship with both the local Arab and Christian populations which was impossible for the American or British contingents to emulate.

There was much public and official congratulation when the boys finally came home. 'Had they been scared?' reporters asked them after they dis-embarked at Livorno. 'Terrified,' was the general consensus of the volunteer force, average age twenty. None was ashamed of publicly admitting fear.

Are Italians improvident and feckless when it comes to looking after collective, as apart from individual, interests?

Take the case of road safety. Despite the accidental deaths each year on the roads of more than two thousand motorcyclists, mostly under twenty-five, it is still not obligatory in Italy to wear a protective crash-helmet for all those riding two-wheeled motorised vehicles, as it is in practically every other European country. No less than sixteen attempts to bring in legislation making crash-helmets compulsory have been blocked in parliament by pressure groups from the motorcycle industry, which fears that there will be an immediate drop in sales if such a law is passed. Italy is also one of the few countries in the developed world where there is no routine alcohol test for motorists suspected of driving under the influence of drink.

Although Italy is, geologically speaking, one of the most unstable countries in Europe, with heavy damage each year being caused through earthquakes, landslides and floods, little attention is paid by the authorities to long-term Public Works projects aimed at circumscribing the effects of such acts of God. Government expenditure on geological services is forty times less than in countries such as Britain or France, with far less serious land subsidence problems. Houses continue to be built without planning permission on the very slopes of active volcanoes, Etna and Vesuvius. Nuclear power stations are planned at sites near seismologically dangerous areas.

The scientific conservation of Italy's vast artistic patrimony is a matter that exercises the conscience of few Italians, despite the dedication of people like Leonetto Tintori. More than a decade after a law was passed to save Venice from crumbling into the Adriatic sea, and two decades after a high water which almost swamped the city once and for all, plans to strengthen Venice's defences against the sea are still being discussed, not implemented. An international competition has been held on how to check the incline of the leaning tower of Pisa, but ever so imperceptibly the tower keels further over each year, as it has done for centuries. Scaffolding encloses many of the monuments of ancient Rome, but inadequate funds have been voted to complete the work of restoration.

With all its accumulations of unfinished business, however, Italy remains for me a country not only of the past, but also psychologically well equipped for the future. Let me explain.

Italians have within the space of only forty years gone through social transformations that have taken place in Britain over a period of more than a hundred and fifty years. Italy has progressed in one swoop from an agricultural to a post-industrial society. This has created immense problems of adaptation for its fifty-six million inhabitants, who, on the whole, have emerged healthier, wealthier, and better educated than ever before in their history.

The enterprise of Italians appears to know no limits. The founder of what is today Italy's biggest publising house could himself neither read nor write adequately. But he was a shrewd judge of character in selecting his staff and his authors, and an excellent businessman in perceiving what sort of reading matter would appeal to people only just emerging from illiteracy like himself.

Italy in the eighties is suffering from severe growing pains. But the country, geographically poised as it is between the developing and the developed worlds, seems to me to have a unique vocation of showing other less gifted nations how, to use Curzio Malaparte's words, 'a people with nothing is capable of everything'.

Do not forget that it was an Italian, Baldassare Castiglione, who first taught the rest of Europe good court manners, and that Italian styles of dress, speech, food, architecture, painting, music and theatre have for centuries influenced and often led the rest of the world.

In the bare statistical terms beloved by economists, Italy is not particularly well endowed. Much of the country is mountainous, unfit for profitable agriculture. It is rich neither in petroleum nor minerals.

But in human resources, Italians can hold their own in any company. As far as I am concerned, the ambiguities and failings of Italy are but a faithful reflection of the ambiguities and failings of the human condition. My years in Italy have taught me to appreciate and savour the qualities of a people who know that culture is not something you acquire, but something you are.

Index